**HOLD**

**SECURE (LOCKOUT)**

**LOCKDOWN**

**EVACUATE**

**SHELTER**

**REUNIFY**

# THE STANDARD RESPONSE PROTOCOL TOOLKIT

# K12 &

# THE STANDARD REUNIFICATION METHOD

# SRM

A General Guide on Incorporating and Operating
The Standard Response Protocol and
The Standard Reunification Method
within a School Safety Plan

**i love u guys**
FOUNDATION

**TEXAS ★ STATE**
Texas School Safety Center

# STANDARD RESPONSE PROTOCOL

## SRP V2.2 CHANGE HISTORY

| AUTHOR/CONTRIBUTOR | VERSION | REVISION DATE | REVISION COMMENTARY |
|---|---|---|---|
| John-Michael Keyes | 1.0 | 03/02/2009 | Original content |
| Russ Deffner<br>John-Michael Keyes | 2.0 | 01/08/2015 | Version update. See: The Standard Response Protocol V2: An Overview of What's New in the SRP |
| Tom Kelley (TxSSC) | 2.1 | 12/02/2017 | Content, edits and Toolkit compliance |
| Texas School Safety Center | 2.2 | 06/05/2020 | Texas-specific content |
| Ellen Stoddard Keyes<br>John-Michael Keyes | 2.3 | 10/05/2021 | Replace Lockout with Secure (Lockout) |

## THE TEXAS SCHOOL SAFETY CENTER

The Texas School Safety Center (TxSSC) is an official university-level research center at Texas State University. The TxSSC is tasked in Chapter 37 of the Texas Education Code and the Governor's Homeland Security Strategic Plan with key school safety initiatives and mandates. Specifically, the TxSSC serves as a clearinghouse for the dissemination of safety and security information through research, training, and technical assistance for K-12 schools and junior colleges throughout the state of Texas. In addition, the TxSSC also builds partnerships among youth, adults, schools, law enforcement officers, and community stakeholders to reduce the impact of tobacco on all Texans through prevention, training and enforcement initiatives.

### MISSION

The Texas School Safety Center serves schools and communities to create safe, secure, and healthy environments.

### VISION

The Texas School Safety Center envisions a world where all schools and communities are safe, secure, and healthy.

## THE "I LOVE U GUYS" FOUNDATION

On September 27th, 2006 a gunman entered Platte Canyon High School in Bailey, Colorado, held seven girls hostage and ultimately shot and killed Emily Keyes. During the time she was held hostage, Emily sent her parents text messages... "I love you guys" and "I love u guys. k?"

Emily's kindness, spirit, fierce joy, and the dignity and grace that followed this tragic event define the core of The "I Love U Guys" Foundation.

### MISSION

The "I Love U Guys" Foundation was created to restore and protect the joy of youth through educational programs and positive actions in collaboration with families, schools, communities, organizations and government entities.

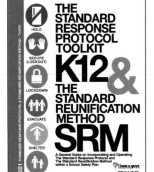

**The Standard Response Protocol Toolkit and Standard Reunification Method**
The "I Love U Guys" Foundation
Texas School Safety Center

ISBN: 978-1-951260-05-7

## COMMITMENT

There are several things we are committed to. The most important thing we can do is offer our material at no cost to schools, districts, departments, agencies and organizations. The reason we are able to continue to provide this service is due, in part, to the generosity of our donors. The "I Love U Guys" Foundation works very hard to keep our costs down as well as any costs associated with our printed materials. Donor support allows us to stretch those dollars and services even more. Your gift, no matter the size, helps us achieve our mission.

Please visit www.iloveuguys.org and donate now. Your help makes a difference to our students, teachers, first responders, and the communities in which we live and work.

## TERMS OF USE

Schools, districts, departments, agencies and organizations may use these materials, at no cost, under the following conditions:

1. Materials are not re-sold.
2. Core actions and directives are not modified.
   2.1. Hold - "In Your Room or Area. Clear the Halls"
   2.2. Secure (Lockout) -"Get Inside, Lock Outside Doors"
   2.3. Lockdown - "Locks, Lights, Out of Sight"
   2.4. Evacuate - A Location may be specified
   2.5. Shelter - followed by the Hazard and the Safety Strategy
3. The Notification of Intent (NOI) is used when the materials are being evaluated. A sample NOI can be downloaded from the website, and is provided to The "I Love U Guys" Foundation through one of the following:
   3.1. Complete the NOI and email it to srp@iloveuguys.org
   3.2. Send an email to srp@iloveuguys.org
4. The Memorandum of Understating (MOU) is used when it has been determined that the materials will be used. A sample MOU can be downloaded from the website, and is provided to The "I Love U Guys" Foundation by emailing it to srp@iloveuguys.org
5. The following modifications to the materials are allowable:
   5.1. Localization of evacuation events
   5.2. Localization of shelter events
   5.3. Addition of organization logo

The "I Love U Guys" Foundation is committed to providing its programs at no cost to a widening variety of organizations.

To assess the fidelity of implementation within an organization, the Foundation has developed a certification program for the Standard Reunification Method. The certification program is optional and is not required to use the SRM within your organization.

## COPYRIGHTS AND TRADEMARKS

## WARNINGS AND DISCLAIMER

## WHAT'S NEW

Texas-specific guidance and mandates have been incorporated into these materials.

## AUTHOR/CONTRIBUTOR INFORMATION

John-Michael Keyes - Primary Author
The "I Love U Guys" Foundation
Executive Director

Russell Deffner - Contributing Author
The "I Love U Guys" Foundation
Advisor/Contractor/Volunteer

Tom Kelley - Contributing Author
Texas School Safety Center
School Safety Specialist

Celina Bley - Texas-specific content and editing
Texas School Safety Center

## SPECIAL THANKS

Pat Hamilton - Executive Director of Operations, Adams 12 Five Star Schools

John McDonald – Executive Director, Safety, Security and Emergency Planning, Jefferson County Public Schools, Colorado

Joleen Reefe - City and County of Broomfield (Joleen coined the phrase, "Locks, Lights, Out of Sight.")

Heidi Walts – Commander, Northglenn Police Department, Colorado

Marta Alejandro – Spanish teacher and bilingual educational support professional / Spanish translator and interpreter

## CONTACT INFORMATION

The "I Love U Guys" Foundation materials are online at http://iloveuguys.org.

Email: info@iloveuguys.org.

The "I Love U Guys" Foundation
PO Box 919
Conifer, CO 80433
303.426.3100

**Executive Director**
John-Michael Keyes
johnmichael@iloveuguys.org

**Mission Director**
Carly Posey
carly@iloveuguys.org

**Operations Director**
Ellen Stoddard-Keyes
ellen@iloveuguys.org

# "Tactics are intel driven."
*What we plan is based on what we know.*

# "But the environment dictates tactics."
*But what we do, is based on where we are.*

**– Sergeant A.J. DeAndrea**
*– Civilian Translation: John-Michael Keyes*

# STANDARD RESPONSE PROTOCOL

## ABOUT THIS BOOK

Since 2015, The Foundation offered optional classroom training that included "Hold in your classroom." In 2017, The Foundation developed materials for The Standard Response Protocol Extended (SRP-X) that included the Hold action.

For SRP 2021, the Hold action is incorporated into the Standard Response Protocol.

Also for SRP 2021, the Action "Lockout" is being changed to Secure. For the purpose of consistency, you will see those words used together in this version.

As you begin to implement and drill the protocol, keep in mind that environments are different. What that means is that we provide you with some tactics. Things we know. But your school, your agencies, and your environment, will ultimately dictate what you do.

Please, in your planning, if you see something here that doesn't seem to work in your environment, figure out what does. Let us know.

# STANDARD RESPONSE PROTOCOL

## REQUEST FOR COMMENT

The Standard Response Protocol is a synthesis of common practices in use at a number of districts, departments and agencies. The evolution of SRP has included review, comment and suggestion from a number of practitioners. As of 2020, the SRP has been subjected to tactical scrutiny by hundreds of law enforcement agencies and operational review an adoption by thousands of schools.

Suggestions for modification can be made via email at srp_rfc@iloveuguys.org. Please include contact information, district, department or agency, including day time phone.

## SRP REVIEW COMMITTEE

The "I Love U Guys" Foundation SRP Review Committee is comprised of safety stakeholders from a variety of perspectives and professions. The charter of the committee is to advise on the merits of any substantive changes to The Standard Response Protocol. This ensures that changes will not be incorporated into the SRP without consideration or deliberation.

The SRP Review Committee communicates on substantive changes to the SRP primarily through electronic means using email or teleconference.

The following are the current members of the SRP Review Committee.

**Dr. David Benke**
The "I Love U Guys" Foundation – Littleton, CO

**Celina Bley**
The Texas School Safety Center - San Marcos, TX

**Pat Hamilton**
Director of Safe and Secure Environments Adams 12 Five Star Schools – Thornton, CO

**John-Michael Keyes**
Executive Director, The "I Love U Guys" Foundation – Conifer, CO

## THE TOOLKIT

This Toolkit was created based on the Standard Response Protocol K12 Operational Guidance created by The "I Love U Guys" Foundation.

The "I Love U Guys" Foundation also provides the ability to order the K12 guides as professionally printed and bound educational materials through Amazon for a cost.

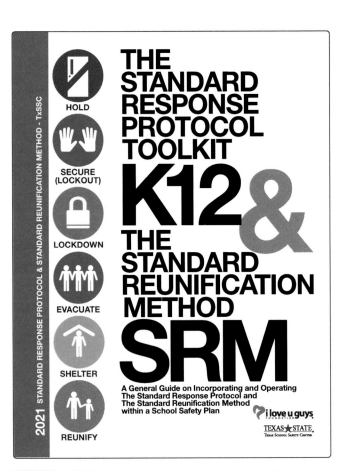

# TABLE OF CONTENTS

# STANDARD RESPONSE PROTOCOL

## 1.0 INTRODUCTION

The K-12 Standard Response Protocol (SRP) Toolkit offers guidance and resources for incorporating the Standard Response Protocol into a school safety plan for critical incident response within individual schools in a school district.

The intent of this toolkit is to provide basic guidance with respect for local conditions and authorities. The only mandate presented is that districts, agencies and departments retain the defined "Terms of Art" and "Directives."

SRP is not a replacement for school safety plans, rather it is a classroom response enhancement for critical incidents designed to provide consistent, clear, shared language and actions among students, staff and first responders.

As a standard, SRP is being adopted by emergency managers, law enforcement, school and district administrators and emergency medical services across the country. Hundreds of agencies have evaluated the SRP and recommended it to thousands of schools.

### TEXAS EDITION

The SRP Toolkit "Texas Edition" was created in conjunction with The "I Love U Guys" Foundation with the intent of incorporating Texas specific guidance and mandates into these processes and materials. This SRP 2021 edition incorporates the former 2017 SRP-X addition of "Hold" and the Action "Lockout" is being changed to "Secure (Lockout)". For the purpose of consistency, you will see those words used together in this version. Texas has mandated drills that school districts and open-enrollment charter schools must follow. They are:

| Drill Type | Frequency |
| --- | --- |
| Secure (Lockout) | 1 per school year |
| Lockdown | 2 per school year<br>- 1 per semester |
| Evacuate | 1 per school year |
| Shelter-In-Place (for hazmat) | 1 per school year |
| Shelter for Severe Weather | 1 per school year |
| Fire Evacuation* | 4 per school year<br>- 2 per semester |

*In addition, school districts and open-enrollment charter schools should consult with their local fire marshal and comply with their local fire marshal's requirements and recommendations.*

Please note that "Hold" is not a mandated drill per Texas Education Code 37.114 and the Texas Education Agency Commissioner's rules. However, "Hold" is considered an "I Love U Guys" best practice drill.

## BEFORE YOU BEGIN

Texas School Districts, Charter Schools and Junior College Districts are required by statute to have a multi-hazard emergency operations plan. School districts and open-enrollment charter schools are also required to have a safety and security committee. The safety and security committee should evaluate if drills are incorporated into the EOP and are conducted at every facility. The committee should also evaluate if substitutes are trained in drills and emergency situations and are taking place throughout the year as substitutes are hired.

Texas law requires that the multi-hazard emergency operation plan provide for measures to ensure coordination with the Texas Department of State Health Services and local emergency management agencies, law enforcement, health departments, and fire departments. This coordination can help ensure safety plans will not conflict with existing local emergency services protocols.

## A CRITICAL LOOK

Be prepared to look at existing plans with a critical eye as often they can be described as a "Directive" of a certain "Term of Art"; i.e. conducting a fire drill is practicing a specific type of evacuation and the actions performed are similar in all evacuation scenarios. It makes sense to teach and train broader evacuation techniques while testing or practicing a more specific directive, like evacuating to the parking lot due to a fire.

## TIME BARRIERS

Time barriers or actions taken beforehand to 'harden the structure' can be an invaluable asset to safety; not only of staff and students, but also visitors to a campus who expect a friendly and secure environment.

Time barriers are best described as a physical barrier that slows down the entry into or movement through a facility. This delay may allow trained persons to take further protective action and gives first responders more time to arrive.

A simple example of a time barrier would be making the exterior doors of a building automatically lock and could include installing a film on glass door panels to prevent them from shattering, delaying an intruder's attempt to break into the premises.

Finally, the most powerful time barrier in an active assailant event is a locked classroom door. The Sandy Hook Advisory Commission Report, issued on March 6, 2015 ( Document page 238 - Appendix A-I.1), states:

*The testimony and other evidence presented to the Commission reveals that there has never been an event in which an active shooter breached a locked classroom door.\**

Investigation into past school shootings reveals only two cases where a person behind a locked classroom door has been physically harmed. In the Red Lake, Minnesota incident, the gunman gained entry to the classroom by means of the side window by the classroom door. In the Platte Canyon, Colorado incident, the gunman was already in the room with hostages when law enforcement explosively breached the classroom door.

## THE STANDARD RESPONSE PROTOCOL

A critical ingredient in the safe school recipe is the uniform classroom response to an incident at school. Weather events, fires, accidents, intruders and other threats to student safety are scenarios that are planned and trained for by school and district administration and staff.

Historically, schools have taken this scenario-based approach to respond to hazards and threats. It's not uncommon to find a stapled sheaf of papers or even a tabbed binder in a teacher's desk that describes a variety of things that might happen and the specific response to each event.

## SRP IS ACTION BASED

The Standard Response Protocol is based not on individual scenarios but on the response to any given scenario. Like the Incident Command System (ICS), SRP demands a specific vocabulary but also allows for great flexibility. The premise is simple – there are five specific actions that can be performed during an incident. When communicating these actions, the action is labeled with a "Term of Art" and is then followed by a "Directive". Execution of the action is performed by active participants, including students, staff, teachers and first responders.

1. **Hold** is followed by a location such as "in your room or area" and is used to clear a specific area, or hallways, in order to manage a situation.

2. **Secure (Lockout)** is followed by: "Get Inside. Lock outside doors" and is the protocol used to safeguard students and staff within the building when there is a nearby threat.

3. **Lockdown** is followed by "Locks, Lights, Out of Sight" and is the protocol used to secure individual rooms and keep students quiet and in place when there is a threat inside the building.

4. **Evacuate** is followed by a location, and is used to move students and staff from one location to a different location in or out of the building when the building needs to be cleared.

5. **Shelter** is always followed by the hazard and a safety strategy and is the protocol for group- and self-protection.

These specific actions can act as both a verb and a noun. If the action is Lockdown, it would be announced on public address as "Lockdown! Locks, Lights, Out of Sight." Communication to local Law Enforcement Agency would then be "We are under Lockdown."

Each response has specific student and staff action. The Evacuate response is always followed by a location: "Evacuate to the Bus Zone." Responses can also be chained. For instance, "Evacuate to Hallway. Shelter for Tornado. Drop, Cover and Hold."

## BENEFITS

The benefits of SRP become quickly apparent. By standardizing the vocabulary, all stakeholders can understand the response and status of the event. For students, this provides continuity of expectations and actions throughout their educational career. For teachers, this becomes a simpler process to train and drill. For first responders, the common vocabulary and protocols establish a greater predictability that persists through the duration of an incident. Parents can easily understand the practices and can reinforce the protocol. Additionally, this protocol enables rapid response determination when an unforeseen event occurs.

The protocol also allows for a more predictable series of actions as an event unfolds. An intruder event may start as a Lockdown, but as the intruder is isolated, first responders would assist as parts of the school go to an "Evacuate to the Gym and Lockdown," and later "Evacuate to the Bus Zone."

## SECURE (LOCKOUT) VS LOCKDOWN

The differentiation between Secure (Lockout) and Lockdown is a critical element in SRP. A Secure (Lockout) action recovers all students and adults from outside the building, secures the building perimeter and locks all outside doors. This would be implemented when there is a threat or hazard outside of the building. Criminal activity, dangerous events in the community, or even a vicious dog on the playground would be examples of a Secure (Lockout) response. While the Secure (Lockout) response encourages greater staff situational awareness, it allows for educational practices to continue with little classroom interruption or distraction.

Lockdown is a classroom-based protocol that requires locking the classroom door, turning off the lights and placing students out of sight of any corridor windows. Student action during Lockdown is to remain quiet. It does not mandate locking exterior doors. There are several reasons for not locking exterior doors during a Lockdown. Risk is increased to students or staff in exposed areas attempting to lock the doors, and locking outside doors inhibits entry of first responders and increases risk as responders attempt to breach doors.

There may be situations where both Lockdown and Secure need to be performed, but in this case they are identified individually. " Secure! Get Inside. Lock outside doors. Lockdown! Locks, Lights, out of Sight." would be announced on public address. We are in "Lockdown and Secure" would be conveyed to emergency services or 911.

## TACTICAL RESPONSES

SRP also acknowledges that some school incidents involve a tactical response from law enforcement, and suggests consultation with local law enforcement regarding expectations and actions.

# 1.1 SRP IN A NUTSHELL

### 5 ACTIONS
The Standard Response Protocol has specific staff and student actions that are unique to the action. In the event student or staff identifies the initial threat, calling 911 and administration is advised.

## SRP OVERVIEW WALL POSTER
This K12 SRP overview wall poster was created to print and place on walls in order to remind everyone of the different SRP actions and allow teachers to start the conversation about SRP with their students.

Placing posters is an essential step in full implementation of the SRP. The classroom poster should be displayed in every classroom, near all entries, and near the entrances to cafeteria, auditorium and gym. The shelter hazards and safety strategies should be modified for local conditions.

### HOLD
**"In Your Room or Area. Clear the halls."**

**Students** are trained to:
- Clear the hallways and remain in their room or area until the "All Clear" is announced
- Do business as usual

**Adults and Staff** are trained to:
- Close and lock the door
- Account for students and adults
- Do business as usual

### SECURE (LOCKOUT)
**"Get Inside. Lock outside doors"**

**Students** are trained to:
- Return to inside of building
- Do business as usual

**Adults and Staff** are trained to:
- Bring everyone indoors
- Lock outside doors
- Increase situational awareness
- Account for students and adults
- Do business as usual

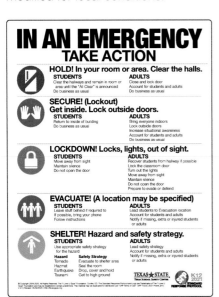

## ONE DEMAND
The protocol also carries an obligation. Kids and teens are smart. An implicit part of the SRP is that authorities and teachers tell them what's going on.

Certainly, tempered at the elementary school. But middle school and above needs accurate information for the greatest survivability, to minimize panic and to assist recovery.

## "AN IMPLICIT PART OF THE SRP IS THAT AUTHORITIES AND TEACHERS TELL THE STUDENTS WHAT'S GOING ON"

*Note: Student training includes preparation for some alternative methods during a tactical response but reinforces deference to local law enforcement.*

## LOCKDOWN
**"Locks, Lights, Out of Sight"**

**Students** are trained to:
- Move away from sight
- Maintain silence
- Do not open the door

**Adults and Staff** are trained to:
- Recover students from hallway if possible
- Lock the classroom door
- Turn out the lights
- Move away from sight
- Maintain silence
- Do not open the door
- Prepare to evade or defend

## EVACUATE
**"To a Location"**

**Students** are trained to:
- Leave stuff behind if required to
- If possible, bring their phone
- Follow instructions

**Adults and Staff** are trained to:
- Bring roll sheet and Go Bag (unless instructed not to take anything with them, dependent on reason for evacuation.)
- Lead students to Evacuation location
- Account for students and adults
- Report injuries or problems using Red Card/ Green Card method.

## SHELTER
**"For Hazard Using a Safety Strategy"**

**Hazards** might include:
- Tornado
- Hazmat
- Earthquake
- Tsunami

**Safety Strategies** might include:
- Evacuate to shelter area
- Seal the room
- Drop, cover and hold
- Get to high ground

**Students** are trained in:
- Appropriate Hazards and Safety Strategies

**Adults and Staff** are trained in:
- Appropriate Hazards and Safety Strategies
- Accounting for students and adults
- Reporting injuries or problems using Red Card/ Green Card method.

### THE DURATION OF A LOCKDOWN

A question that occasionally arises is "How long does it take to release a Lockdown?" The answer is, "That depends, but probably longer than you want to hear."

The Foundation has heard accounts of a Lockdown lasting for hours. In the case of a weapon report, the school was in Lockdown for over three hours. In another, an active shooter in the building, it took about an hour after the issue was resolved for law enforcement to clear the classrooms.

Some schools have created Lockdown kits. A five gallon bucket, kitty litter, and a shower curtain to accommodate the potential of being unable to use a restroom.

### WHAT ABOUT CELL PHONES?

One of the occasionally heated conversations is about cell phone usage. If the current trends continue, there will be a point in the future where nearly every student will have a device. Not just middle and high school, but elementary as well.

There may be cases where law enforcement will ask students to leave their phones behind. A bomb threat for example.

In many cases, having the ability to craft messages for students to send their parents, or for students to call their parents, can be of tremendous value.

The Foundation freely admits to a bias though. Take just a moment and think of the origination of the Foundation. (See page 4.)

### ABOUT SHELTER-IN-PLACE

Traditionally, the term "Shelter-in-place" is used for a variety of hazards. While still in common use, the SRP suggests stating the hazard and providing a safety strategy.

The FEMA website has over a dozen different scenarios for "Shelter-in-place." Two of the most common were for Tornado or Hazmat. Very different actions would be taken for those hazards.

A single directive, "Shelter-in-place," doesn't provide the necessary information. "Tornado! Get to the storm shelter!" is more direct.

# 1.2 PROTOCOL DETAILS

## SUMMARY

This section of the guidance defines conditions, actions responsibilities and other aspects of preparing and incorporating The Standard Response Protocol within a school or district safety plan.

# PREREQUISITES

## NIMS AND ICS

In order to coordinate the use of the SRP in district plans, it is highly recommended that key individuals within the district and those with a role in district/campus emergency operations, complete the following courses through FEMA.

1. IS 100.C: Introduction to the Incident Command System
2. IS-700.B: An Introduction to the National Incident Management System
3. IS 362.A: Multihazard Emergency Planning for Schools

These courses are available online, at no cost using the web at http://training.fema.gov. Anticipate 1 to 3 hours per course to successfully achieve certification. The courses are offered at no charge. Please note: The "I Love U Guys" Foundation is not affiliated with FEMA.

## CREATING TIME BARRIERS

Historical data on active shooters suggests that a locked classroom door is a proven life-saving strategy. Barricading is another option that has a positive track record. These strategies all provide a "Time Barrier" between people and potential assailants.

## DOORS, LOCKS, AND STRESS

A consistent observation by first responders is that human beings have difficulty completing even routine tasks when they are under stress. The otherwise simple task of locking the classroom door may become extremely difficult for a teacher who has just heard a Lockdown order. Elevated adrenaline levels may result in the loss of fine motor skills and often result in difficulty even inserting a key into a door lock.

Keeping classroom doors locked during instruction has proven to be a time barrier. While this may create an inconvenience if students are late or need to re-enter classroom for other reasons, it provides an essential layer of protection against intruders.

## TALK TO THE FIRE MARSHAL

It's important to discuss classroom security options and modification with local fire authorities. Variances in local Fire Codes and application may determine if it is an option for your schools.

## MEMORANDA OF UNDERSTANDING

Establishing a Memorandum of Understanding (MOU) and/or Mutual Aid Agreement (MAA) between responding agencies and local resources are critical. It is insufficient to rely on a conversation or handshake between entities who would respond to an incident or provide resources during an emergency.

Written agreements such as MOUs and MAAs are important to emergency operation plans and should be reviewed and updated regularly.

> **"ESTABLISHING A MEMORANDUM OF UNDERSTANDING BETWEEN STAKEHOLDERS IS CRITICAL."**

An SRP-focused Sample MOU between a School District and Law Enforcement/Fire/EMS was created by The "I Love U Guys" Foundation in order to guide schools in creating effective MOU's with local first responders. This can be downloaded from The "I Love U Guys" Foundation's website.

## THE "I LOVE U GUYS" FOUNDATION MOUs OR NOTICE OF INTENT

Some schools, districts, departments and agencies may also desire a formalized Memorandum of Understanding (MOU) with The "I Love U Guys" Foundation. Please visit https://iloveuguys.org for a current version of the MOU. The purpose of this MOU is to define responsibilities of each party and provide scope, clarity of expectations. It affirms agreement of stated protocol by schools, districts, departments and agencies. It also confirms the online availability of the Foundation's materials.

An additional benefit for the Foundation is in seeking funding. Some private grantors view the MOU as a demonstration of program effectiveness.

Another option is to formally notify the Foundation with a Notice of Intent (NOI). This is a notice that you are reviewing the materials but have not adopted them yet. This is also available on the website.

At a minimum, schools, districts, departments and agencies that will ultimately incorporate the SRP into their safety plans and practices should email srp@iloveuguys.org and let them know.

# STANDARD RESPONSE PROTOCOL

## 2.0 THE SRP ACTIONS

The Standard Response Protocol (SRP) is based on an all-hazards approach as opposed to individual scenarios. Like the Incident Command System (ICS), SRP utilizes clear common language while allowing for flexibility in protocol. The premise is simple - there are five specific actions that can be performed during an incident. When communicating these, the action is labeled with a "Term of Art" and is then followed by a "Directive." Execution of the action is performed by active participants, including students, staff, teachers and first responders. The SRP is based on the following actions: Hold, Secure, Lockdown, Evacuate and Shelter.

## SRP STUDENT PARENT HANDOUT

This K12 SRP Student Parent Handout was created by The "I Love U Guys" Foundation for you to print and send home with your students in order to inform parents that your school is using the SRP and to educate parents on the protocol actions. This includes some useful information for parents about what to expect during a Secure or Lockout drills or incidents.

The Parent Handout is useful in implementing the SRP. Many districts request that their schools send this home with students at the beginning of the school year and again prior to any planned drill.

---

### STANDARD RESPONSE PROTOCOL

#### INFORMATION FOR PARENTS AND GUARDIANS
Our school has adopted The "I Love U Guys" Foundation's Standard Response Protocol (SRP). Students and staff will be training, practicing, and drilling the protocol.

#### COMMON LANGUAGE
The Standard Response Protocol (SRP) is based on an all-hazards approach as opposed to individual scenarios. Like the Incident Command System (ICS), SRP utilizes clear common language while allowing for flexibility in protocol.

The premise is simple - there are five specific actions that can be performed during an incident. When communicating these, the action is labeled with a "Term of Art" and is then followed by a "Directive." Execution of the action is performed by active participants, including students, staff, teachers and first responders. The SRP is based on the following actions: Hold, Secure (Lockout), Lockdown, Evacuate, and Shelter.

#### HOLD
"In Your Room or Area. Clear the Halls."

**Students** are trained to:
- Clear the hallways and remain in their room or area until the "All Clear" is announced
- Do business as usual

**Adults and staff** are trained to:
- Close and lock the door
- Account for students and adults
- Do business as usual

#### SECURE
(Lockout)
"Get Inside. Lock outside doors"

**Students** are trained to:
- Return to inside of building
- Do business as usual

**Adults and staff** are trained to:
- Bring everyone indoors
- Lock outside doors
- Increase situational awareness
- Account for students and adults
- Do business as usual

#### LOCKDOWN
"Locks, Lights, Out of Sight"

**Students** are trained to:
- Move away from sight
- Maintain silence
- Do not open the door

**Adults and staff** are trained to:
- Recover students from hallway if possible
- Lock the classroom door
- Turn out the lights
- Move away from sight
- Maintain silence
- Do not open the door
- Prepare to evade or defend

#### EVACUATE
"To a Location"

**Students** are trained to:
- Leave stuff behind if required to
- If possible, bring their phone
- Follow instructions

**Adults and staff** are trained to:
- Bring roll sheet and Go Bag (unless instructed not to take anything with them, dependent on reason for evacuation.)
- Lead students to Evacuation location
- Account for students and adults
- Report injuries or problems using Red Card/Green Card method.

#### SHELTER
"State Hazard and Safety Strategy"

**Hazards** might include:
- Tornado
- Hazmat
- Earthquake
- Tsunami

**Safety Strategies** might include:
- Evacuate to shelter area
- Seal the room
- Drop, cover and hold
- Get to high ground

**Students** are trained in:
- Appropriate Hazards and Safety Strategies

**Adults and staff** are trained in:
- Appropriate Hazards and Safety Strategies
- Accounting for students and adults
- Reporting injuries or problems using Red Card/Green Card method.

---

### STANDARD RESPONSE PROTOCOL

#### PARENT GUIDANCE
In the event of a live incident, parents may have questions about their role.

#### SECURE (LOCKOUT)
"Get Inside. Lock outside doors"

Secure was formerly called Lockout, and the actions are the same. It is called when there's something dangerous outside of the building. Students and staff are brought into the building and the outside doors will be locked. The school might display the Building is Secured poster on entry doors or nearby windows. Inside, it will be business as usual.

#### SHOULD PARENTS COME TO THE SCHOOL DURING A SECURE (LOCKOUT) EVENT?
Probably not. Every effort is made to conduct classes as normal during a secure event. Additionally, parents may be asked to stay outside during a Secure event.

#### WHAT IF PARENTS NEED TO PICK UP THEIR STUDENT?
Depending on the situation, it may not be safe to release the student. As the situation evolves, Secure (Lockout) might change to a Monitored Entry and/or Controlled Release.

#### WILL PARENTS BE NOTIFIED WHEN A SCHOOL GOES INTO SECURE?
When a Secure (Lockout) condition is brief or the hazard is non-violent, like a wild animal on the playground, there may not be a need to notify parents while the Secure is in place. With longer or more dangerous events, the school should notify parents that the school has increased their security.

#### LOCKDOWN
"Locks, Lights, Out of Sight"

A Lockdown is called when there is something dangerous inside of the building. Students and staff are trained to enter or remain in a room that can be locked, and maintain silence.

A Lockdown is only initiated when there is an active threat inside or very close to the building.

**SCHOOL IS SECURED**
MONITORED ENTRY AND CONTROLLED RELEASE

**ESCUELA BAJO PROTECCIÓN**
ENTRADA VIGILADA Y SALIDA CONTROLADA

#### SHOULD PARENTS COME TO THE SCHOOL DURING A LOCKDOWN?
The natural inclination for parents is to go to the school during a Lockdown. Understandable, but perhaps problematic. If there is a threat inside the building, law enforcement will be responding. It is unlikely that parents will be granted access to the building or even the campus. If parents are already in the school, they will be instructed to Lockdown as well.

#### SHOULD PARENTS TEXT THEIR STUDENTS?
The school recognizes the importance of communication between parents and students during a Lockdown event. Parents should be aware though, during the initial period of a Lockdown, it may not be safe for students to text their parents. As the situation resolves, students may be asked to update their parents on a regular basis.

In some cases, students may be evacuated and transported off-site for a student-parent reunification.

#### WHAT ABOUT UNANNOUNCED DRILLS?
The school may conduct unscheduled drills, however it is highly discouraged to conduct one without announcing that it as a drill. That's called an unannounced drill and can cause undue concern and stress.

**DRILL IN PROGRESS NO ONE IN OR OUT**

**SIMULACRO EN CURSO NO SE PERMITE LA ENTRADA O SALIDA DE NADIE**

Parents should recognize that the school will always inform students that it is a drill during the initial announcement.

It's important to differentiate between a **drill** and an exercise. A drill is used to create the "muscle memory" associated with a practiced action. There is no simulation of an event, simply performing the action. An exercise simulates an actual event to test the capacity of personnel and equipment.

#### CAN PARENTS OBSERVE OR PARTICIPATE IN THE DRILLS?
The school welcomes parents who wish to observe or participate in drills.

**TEXAS ★ STATE**
TEXAS SCHOOL SAFETY CENTER

---

# 2.1 HOLD

## CONDITION

There may be situations that require students to remain in their classrooms or in an area to keep another area clear of people. For example, an altercation in the hallway may demand keeping students out of the halls until it is resolved. There may be a need for students who are not in a classroom to proceed to an area where they can be supervised and remain safe.

## PUBLIC ADDRESS

The public address for Hold is: "Hold in your room or area. Clear the halls." and is repeated twice each time the public address is performed. Be as specific as necessary about the place that needs to be kept clear. Be aware if there is a need to add additional directives for any students that are not in a classroom, at lunch or some other location where they should remain until the hold is lifted.

"Hold in your room or area. Clear the halls."
"Hold in your room or area. Clear the halls."

## PUBLIC ADDRESS - RELEASE

A hold can be released by Public Address.

"The Hold is released. All Clear."

## INCIDENT COMMAND SYSTEM

The School Incident Command System should be initiated.

## ACTIONS

Students and teachers are to remain in their room or area, even if there is a scheduled class change, until the all clear is announced.

Students and staff in common areas, like a cafeteria or a gym, may be asked to remain in those areas or move to adjoining areas like a locker room.

Students and staff outside of the building should remain outside, unless administration directs otherwise.

It is suggested that prior to locking the classroom door, teachers should rapidly sweep the hallway for nearby students. Additionally, teachers should take attendance, note the time, and conduct business as usual.

## RESPONSIBILITY

Typically an administrator is responsible for initiating a Hold, however anyone should be able to call for a Hold if they observe something happening that would require this action.

## PREPARATION

Student, teacher, and administrator training.

## DRILLS

Hold is not a Texas mandated drill, however it is recommended to be drilled at least once per school year.

## CONTINGENCIES

Students are trained that if they are not in a classroom they should try to identify the nearest classroom and join that class for the duration of the Hold.

# 2.2 SECURE (LOCKOUT)

## CONDITION

Secure (Lockout) is called when there is a threat or hazard outside of the school building. Whether it's due to violence or criminal activity in the immediate neighborhood, or a dangerous animal on the playground, Secure (Lockout) uses the security of the physical facility to act as protection.

## PUBLIC ADDRESS

The public address for Secure is: "Secure! Get Inside. Lock outside doors" and is repeated twice each time the public address is performed.

"Secure! Get Inside. Lock outside doors.
 Secure! Get Inside. Lock outside doors."

## INCIDENT COMMAND SYSTEM

The School Incident Command System should be initiated.

## ACTIONS

The Secure (Lockout) protocol demands bringing people into a secure building, locking all outside access points.

Where possible, classroom activities would continue uninterrupted. Classes being held outside would return to the building and, if possible, continue inside the building.

There may be occasions when students expect to be able to leave the building - end of classes, job commitment, etc. Depending on the condition, this may have to be delayed until the area is safe. During the training period, it should be emphasized to students as well as their parents that they may be inconvenienced by these directives, but their cooperation is important to ensure their safety.

## RESPONSIBILITY

In a Secure (Lockout) condition, administration or staff may be required to lock exterior access points. Staff members assigned "Primary Responsibility" for a "Secure Zone" would follow the designated protocol during a drill as well. These areas may include doorways, windows, loading docks, and fire escape ladder access points. The assigned staff is designated as having "Secure Duty."

A person should also be assigned "Secondary Responsibility" for Secure Duty in the event the person with Primary Responsibility is absent or unable to perform the protocol.

Assign someone to place the appropriate "Building is Secure" posters (shown on the right) on the main entry doors so visitors are aware of the situation.

## REPORTED BY

Secure (Lockout) is typically reported by emergency dispatch to the school office. Office staff then invokes the public address and informs administration.

It may also be reported to the school office by students, staff or teachers if a threat is directly observed outside of the building.

# 2.2 SECURE (LOCKOUT)

## PREPARATION

Identification of perimeter access points that must be locked in the event of a Secure (Lockout) defines the Perimeter.

Secure Zones - areas of a school or campus with exterior access points - should be established, and protocols developed, to ensure that those on "Secure Duty" secure all areas in their zone.

Preparation includes identification of staff with Primary and Secondary responsibility and assignment of these duties.

## DRILLS

In Texas, Secure (Lockout) drills must be performed at least once per school year. Schools should consider conducting this drill while outdoor activities are in progress.

## CONTINGENCIES

There may be physical attributes to the campus that mandate special handling of a Secure (Lockout) condition. An example would be a campus where modular buildings are present. If the modular building cannot be secured, it may be best for students to Evacuate to the main building rather than going to a Secure (Lockout) condition in the modular building. Listen for specific additional directives.

If the school is a distributed campus (multiple permanent buildings), they will have to consider what their perimeter is. In a perceived and indirect threat, they may decide that extra supervision for class changes between buildings is sufficient and appropriate.

If during a Secure (Lockout) event an additional hazard manifests i.e.: fire, flood, hazmat, then additional directives will be given for the appropriate response.

## EXAMPLES OF SECURE CONDITIONS

The following are some examples of when a school or emergency dispatch might call for a Secure (Lockout) condition.

- Unknown or unauthorized person on the grounds
- Dangerous animal on school grounds
- Criminal activity in area
- Civil disobedience

## SCHOOL IS SECURED
### NO ONE IN OR OUT

## ESCUELA BAJO PROTECCIÓN
### NADIE PUEDE ENTRAR

TEXAS★STATE.
Texas School Safety Center

© Copyright 2009-2020. All Rights Reserved. The "I Love U Guys" Foundation. Conifer, CO. The Standard Response Protocol and Logo are Trademarks of The "I Love U Guys" Foundation and may be registered in certain j04/16ctions. This material may be duplicated for distribution per "SRP Terms of Use". SRP TxSSC 2021 Secure Door Poster_EN-SP | V 3.0 | Revised: 05/30/2020

## SCHOOL IS SECURED
### MONITORED ENTRY AND CONTROLLED RELEASE

## ESCUELA BAJO PROTECCIÓN
### ENTRADA VIGILADA Y SALIDA CONTROLADA

TEXAS★STATE.
Texas School Safety Center

© Copyright 2009-2020. All Rights Reserved. The "I Love U Guys" Foundation. Conifer, CO. The Standard Response Protocol and Logo are Trademarks of The "I Love U Guys" Foundation and may be registered in certain j04/16ctions. This material may be duplicated for distribution per "SRP Terms of Use". SRP TxSSC Secure Monitored Door Poster_EN-SP | V 3.0 | Revised: 05/30/2020

# 2.3
# LOCKDOWN
### CONDITION

Lockdown is called when there is a threat or hazard inside the school building. From parental custody disputes to intruders to an active assailant, Lockdown uses classroom and school security actions to protect students and staff from the threat.

## PUBLIC ADDRESS

The public address for Lockdown is: "Lockdown! Locks, Lights, Out of Sight!" and is repeated twice each time the public address is performed.

"Lockdown! Locks, Lights, Out of Sight!
Lockdown! Locks, Lights, Out of Sight!"

## INCIDENT COMMAND SYSTEM

The School Incident Command System should be initiated.

## ACTIONS

The Lockdown Protocol demands locking individual classroom doors, offices and other securable areas, moving room occupants out of line of sight of corridor windows and having room occupants maintain silence.

There is no call to action to lock the building outside access points. Rather, the protocol advises to leave the perimeter as is. The reasoning is simple - sending staff to lock outside doors exposes them to unnecessary risk and inhibits first responders' entry into the building.

Teacher, staff and student training reinforces the practice of not opening the classroom door once in Lockdown. Rather, no indication of occupancy should be revealed until administrators or first responders open the door.

If the location of the threat is apparent and people do not have the option to get behind a door, it is appropriate to self-evacuate away from the threat.

## RESPONSIBILITY

The classroom teacher is responsible for implementing their classroom Lockdown. If is safe to do so, the teacher should gather students into the classroom prior to locking door. The teacher should lock all classroom access points and facilitate moving occupants out of sight.

## REPORTED BY

Lockdown is typically reported by students or staff to the school office. The office staff then invokes the public address and informs administration.

It may also be reported to the school office by local emergency dispatch.

## PREPARATION

Identification of classroom access points that must be locked in the event of a Lockdown is essential preparation. These may include doorways, windows, loading docks, and fire escape ladder access points.

A "safe zone" should also be identified within the classroom that is out of sight of the corridor window. Teachers and students should be trained to not open the classroom door, leaving a first responder, school safety team member or school administrator to unlock it.

Students, staff and teachers should be advised that a Lockdown may persist for several hours and during an incident, silence is essential.

## DRILLS

In Texas, Lockdown drills must be performed at least twice per school year, once per semester. If possible one of these drills should be performed with local law enforcement personnel participation. At a minimum, law enforcement participation in the drill should occur no less than once every two years.

For more information see the Lockdown Drills section of this toolkit.

**DRILL IN PROGRESS
NO ONE IN OR OUT**

**SIMULACRO EN CURSO
NO SE PERMITE LA ENTRADA
O SALIDA DE NADIE**

TEXAS★STATE
Texas School Safety Center

## CONTINGENCIES

Students and staff who are outside of classrooms when a Lockdown is announced, should to get into the first classroom with a teacher or that can be secured. In the event someone cannot get into a room before doors are locked, they should be instructed about other options. In this situation students and staff should be trained to hide or even evacuate themselves away from the building or area. Students and staff should receive training on where to go, if they evacuate, so they can be safe and accounted for.

If, during a Lockdown, an additional hazard manifests inside the school such as a fire, flood, or hazmat incident, then situational decisions must be made. There should be discussions about reacting to a fire alarm if it is activated during a Lockdown. This may require following additional directives of the SRP.

## EXAMPLES OF LOCKDOWN CONDITIONS

The following are simply some examples of when a school or emergency dispatch might call for a Lockout.

- Dangerous animal within school building
- Intruder
- Angry or violent parent or student
- Report of a weapon
- Active assailant

## RED CARD/GREEN CARD

Red Card/Green Cards should NOT be used for a lockdown. Based on a number of tactical assessments, the overwhelming consensus is that this practice provides information to an armed intruder that there are potential targets in that room.

# 2.4 EVACUATE
## CONDITION

Evacuate is called when there is a need to move people from one location to another.

Most often, evacuations will be necessary when there's a heating/ventilation system failure, gas leak, or bomb threat in the area. In those cases, people will be allowed to bring their personal items with them. An evacuation drill is very similar to a fire drill.

## PUBLIC ADDRESS

The public address for Evacuate is: "Evacuate! To a Location" and is repeated twice each time the public address is performed. For instance, "Evacuate! To the Flag Pole. Evacuate! To the Flag Pole."

"Evacuate! To a location. Evacuate! To a location."

## INCIDENT COMMAND SYSTEM

The School Incident Command System should be initiated.

## ACTIONS

The Evacuate Protocol demands students and staff move in an orderly fashion.

## RESPONSIBILITY

The classroom teacher or administrator is usually responsible for initiating an evacuation. The directives or actions may vary for fire, bomb threat, or other emergency. In a police led evacuation, students may be instructed to form a single file line and hold hands front and back, or students and staff may be asked to put their hands on their heads while evacuating. Other directions may be invoked during an evacuation and student and staff should be prepared to follow specific instructions given by staff or first responders.

## PREPARATION

Evacuation preparation involves the identification of facility Evacuation Points, as well as student, teacher, and administrator training.

## EVACUATION ASSEMBLY

The Evacuation Assembly refers to gathering at the Evacuation Assembly Point(s). Teachers are instructed to take roll after arrival at the Evacuation Assembly Point(s).

## DRILLS

In Texas, Evacuation drills must be performed at least once per school year. Fire evacuation drills are mandated separately in Texas to four per school year, two per semester. It is recommended that you discuss fire evacuation drills with your local fire marshal to ensure compliance with local fire code.

## INCIDENT COMMAND SYSTEM

The School Incident Command System should be initiated.

## CONTINGENCIES

Students are trained that if they are separated from their class during an evacuation, then joining an evacuation line is acceptable. They should be instructed to identify themselves to the teacher in their group after arriving at the Evacuation site.

## STANDARD REUNIFICATION METHOD

The "I Love U Guys" Foundation has developed guidance for reunifying parents with their children. These materials are available at no cost to districts, departments and agencies.

## RED CARD/GREEN CARD/MED CARD

After taking roll the Red/Green/Med Card system is employed for administration or first responders to quickly, visually identify the status of the teachers' classes.

(Select only one of the three card styles below.)

- Green Card (OK) - All students accounted for, No immediate help is necessary
- Red Card (Help) - Extra or missing students, or vital information must be exchanged
- Red and White Cross (Medical Help) - Immediate medical attention is needed

Schools may opt to use the SRP single sheet advisory which can be folded to any visual indicator.

## RED CARD/GREEN CARD/ROLL CARD

An alternative design to the Red/Green/Med Card is the Red/Green/Roll Card.

## RED CARD/GREEN CARD/ALERT CARD

Another alternative the Red/Green/Alert Card.

# 2.5 SHELTER
## CONDITION

Shelter is called when specific protective actions are needed based on a threat or hazard. Training should include response to threats such as tornado, earthquake or hazmat.

## PUBLIC ADDRESS

The public addresses for shelter should include the hazard and the safety strategy. The public address is repeated twice each time the public address is performed.

"The public addresses for shelter should include the hazard and the safety strategy."

## HAZARDS MAY INCLUDE

- Tornado
- Severe Weather
- Wildfires
- Flooding
- Hazmat spill or release
- Earthquake
- Tsunami

## SAFETY STRATEGIES MAY INCLUDE

- Evacuate to shelter area
- Seal the room
- Drop, cover and hold
- Get to high ground

## ACTIONS

The Texas School Safety Center website contains guidance resources for actions associated with severe weather and other threats. Collaboration with local responders, the national weather service, and other local, regional and state resources should be consulted in developing specific actions for your district response.

**"SHELTER SAFETY STRATEGIES SHOULD BE DRILLED AT LEAST TWICE A YEAR."**

## INCIDENT COMMAND SYSTEM

The School Incident Command System should be initiated.

## RESPONSIBILITY

Sheltering requires all students and staff follow response directives. Districts should have procedures for every hazard and threat which include provisions for those individuals with access and functional needs.

## PREPARATION

Identification and marking of facility shelter areas.

## DRILLS

In Texas, Shelter drills must be held twice per school year; once for a Shelter-In-Place (for hazmat) and one for Shelter in severe weather.

## SHELTER - STATE THE HAZARD AND SAFETY STRATEGY

Using the Shelter directive and stating the hazard, allows for understanding of the threat and the associated protective actions. Most often, shelter directive is utilized for tornadoes or severe weather, in which case the directive would include where students and staff should shelter and be ready to take a protective posture. Sheltering for a Hazmat spill or release, is very different. In the case of a Hazmat situation, students and staff would be directed to close their windows, shut down their heating and air conditioning units and seal windows and doors to preserve the good inside air while restricting the entry of any contaminated outside air. Listening to specific directives is critical to a successful emergency response.

## PLAIN LANGUAGE

NIMS and ICS require the use of plain language. Codes and specific language that are not readily understood by the general public are no longer to be used. The SRP uses shared, plain, natural language between students, staff and first responders. This is evident in the directives provided in the SRP. If there are specific directives that need to be issued for a successful response in a school, those should be made clearly using plain language. There is nothing wrong with adding additional directives as to where to shelter, or what protective actions should be used in the response.

## CUSTOMIZATION

The classroom poster is sufficient for generic Shelter guidance. The Foundation recognizes that localized hazards may need to be added to the poster.

Original, digital artwork can be provided to organizations that have signed a "Notice of Intent" or a "Memorandum of Understanding" with The "I Love U Guys" Foundation.

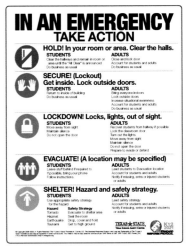

Please note: Depending on the content, original artwork is only provided in the following formats for Mac OS X:
- QuarkXPress® 2019
- Pages 10.0 for Mac OS X, iOS, or iWork for iCloud

Currently, artwork is not available for Microsoft Word.

# 3.0 LOCKDOWN DRILLS
## INTRODUCTION TO LOCKDOWN DRILLS

A critical aspect in implementing the SRP with fidelity is the Lockdown Drill. Successful drills provide participants with the "muscle memory" should an actual Lockdown occur. Drills also reveal deficiencies that may exist in either procedure or personnel.

## PREPARATION

Prior to drilling, students, staff and administration should review the SRP Training Presentation (available at http://iloveuguys.org). Administration should also verify with law enforcement their use of the SRP in the school or district.

Teachers should take time with students to identify and occupy a "Safe Zone" in the classroom where they cannot be seen through any corridor windows. If visibility in a classroom is problematic, window covering or alternative locations should be identified.

Additionally, the following instructions should be delivered to students.

1. Locate yourself at a point in the classroom where you can no longer see out the corridor window.
2. Maintain silence. No cell phone calls.
3. Refrain from texting during drills.

## PARTNERSHIPS

School level drills should have district support. There may also be district resources available to assist in conducting the drill. Another key partnership is with local law enforcement. Local patrol, community resource officers or school resource officers should be part of the drill process.

## THE EMERGENCY RESPONSE TEAM

Some school have a pre-identified Building/School Emergency Response Team. These teams are effective for responding to any type of incident.

It is a noted best practice for administration to survey the staff population for prior emergency response, military or law enforcement experience, and specialized training and skills for use in district emergency operations.

## THE LOCKDOWN DRILL TEAM

During an actual Lockdown, members of the Emergency Response Team may be in classrooms or administrative offices in Lockdown mode and unable to assist with the response.

The Lockdown Drill Team should not include personnel that have specific roles during an actual emergency within that school. Instead, the team might include district safety representatives, law enforcement, and those administrators from another school.

## STAFF NOTIFICATION

When Lockdown Drills are first being introduced to a school, it is absolutely okay to tell staff in advance of the drill. There may be staff members adversely affected by surprise drills.

## SPECIAL NEEDS CONSIDERATIONS

It is critical to identify any specific issues that may cause challenges for students with special needs or disabilities and incorporate appropriate actions for notification prior to drills. It is not recommended that additional assistance be provided in special needs areas for drills, UNLESS this assistance is part of the plan and those resources will be assigned in an actual emergency.

## THE PRE-DRILL BRIEFING

Prior to the Lockdown Drill a short planning meeting with the Lockdown Drill Team should occur. The agenda is simple:

1. Review the floor plan and team member assignments
2. Expected drill duration
3. The door knock and classroom conversation
4. Potential student or staff distress

## ANNOUNCING THE LOCKDOWN DRILL

When using public address to announce a Lockdown Drill, repeat, "Lockdown. Locks, Lights, Out of Sight. This is a drill." It's important to tell students and staff that this is a drill. Failure to do so will most likely result in parents, media and maybe even law enforcement coming to the school.

"Lockdown. Locks, Lights, Out of Sight. This is a drill."

## CONDUCTING THE DRILL

The Lockdown Drill Team should be broken into groups of two or three members who go to individual classrooms. One of the members acts as "Scribe" and documents each classroom response.

At the classroom door, team members listen for noise and look through the corridor window for any student or staff visibility or movement. A team member then knocks on the door and requests entry. There should be no response to this request. At this point a member of the team unlocks the classroom door and announces their name and position.

This Lockdown Response Worksheet was created by The "I Love U Guys" Foundation to assist you in conducting and documenting your lockdown drills.

## THE CLASSROOM CONVERSATION

Typically, this conversation addresses the purpose of the drill, and the observed outcome for that classroom. Additionally, self-evacuation and other life safety strategies can be discussed. Any issues should be addressed gently but immediately.

## WINDOWS

Often there is a conversation about inside and outside windows. Corridor windows are left uncovered so that first responders can see inside the room. Outside windows are left untouched because the threat would be inside the building. There are different preferences regarding window coverings, so please discuss this with your local responders to make sure you're in agreement.

## THE LOCKDOWN DRILL TEAM DEBRIEF

At the conclusion of the drill, the team should reconvene for a debrief. Any issues should be documented, the safety plan reviewed, and actions items identified. An opportunity for all staff to submit information regarding the performance of the drill should be part of the after-action review process.

# THE STANDARD REUNIFICATION METHOD

# SRM V2

**REUNIFY**

**A Practical Method to Unite Students with Parents After an Evacuation or Crisis.**
**The "I Love U Guys" Foundation**

SRM Version 2.0

# STANDARD™
# REUNIFICATION METHOD

## CHANGE HISTORY VERSION 2.0

| AUTHOR/CONTRIBUTOR | VERSION | REVISION DATE | REVISION COMMENTARY |
|---|---|---|---|
| John-Michael Keyes | 0.9.0 | 09/17/2011 | Preliminary Draft |
| John-Michael Keyes | 0.9.1 | 10/01/2011 | First Final Content Revision |
| Ellen Stoddard-Keyes | 0.9.2 | 10/16/2011 | Preliminary Edits |
| Lee Shaughnessy | 0.9.3 | 10/26/2011 | Preliminary Edits |
| Joseph Majsak. SVP & Chief Marketing Officer, Genesis Mgmt. & Ins. Services Corp. | 1.0 | 11/16/2011 | Continuity and Final Edits |
| John-Michael Keyes | 1.1 | 06/08/2016 | Additional Content |
| John-Michael Keyes Will Schwall Michelle Brady Russ Deffner Carolyn Mears | 2.0 | 03/02/2017 | Reunifier replaces Runner Additional Content Edits |

## COMMITMENT

There are several things we are committed to. The most important thing we do is offer our material at no cost to schools, districts, departments, agencies and organizations. The reason we are able to continue to provide this service is due, in part, to the generosity of our donors. The "I Love U Guys" Foundation works very hard to keep our costs down as well as any costs associated with our printed materials. Donor support allows us to stretch those dollars and services even more. Your gift, no matter the size, helps us achieve our mission.

Please visit www.iloveuguys.org and donate now. Your help makes a difference to our students, teachers, first responders, and the communities in which we live and work.

**A Practical Method to Unite Students with Parents After an Evacuation or Crisis**
The "I Love U Guys" Foundation

Version 2.1

TEXAS ★ STATE.
TEXAS SCHOOL SAFETY CENTER

## THE TEXAS SCHOOL SAFETY CENTER

The Texas School Safety Center (TxSSC) is an official university-level research center at Texas State University. The TxSSC is tasked in Chapter 37 of the Texas Education Code and the Governor's Homeland Security Strategic Plan with key school safety initiatives and mandates. Specifically, the TxSSC serves as a clearinghouse for the dissemination of safety and security information through research, training, and technical assistance for K-12 schools and junior colleges throughout the state of Texas. In addition, the TxSSC also builds partnerships among youth, adults, schools, law enforcement officers, and community stakeholders to reduce the impact of tobacco on all Texans through prevention, training and enforcement initiatives.

## MISSION

The Texas School Safety Center serves schools and communities to create safe, secure, and healthy environments.

## VISION

The Texas School Safety Center envisions a world where all schools and communities are safe, secure, and healthy.

## THE "I LOVE U GUYS" FOUNDATION

On September 27th, 2006 a gunman entered Platte Canyon High School in Bailey, Colorado, held seven girls hostage and ultimately shot and killed Emily Keyes. During the time she was held hostage, Emily sent her parents text messages... "I love you guys" and "I love u guys. k?"

Emily's kindness, spirit, fierce joy, and the dignity and grace that followed this tragic event define the core of The "I Love U Guys" Foundation.

## MISSION

The "I Love U Guys" Foundation was created to restore and protect the joy of youth through educational programs and positive actions in collaboration with families, schools, communities, organizations and government entities.

## TERMS OF USE

Schools, districts, departments, agencies and organizations may use these materials, at no cost, under the following conditions:

1. Materials are not re-sold.
2. Notification of use is provided to The "I Love U Guys" Foundation through one of the following:
    2.1. Email notice of use to srm@iloveuguys.org
    2.2. Notice of Intent
    2.3. Memorandum of Understanding
3. The following modification to the materials (handouts, cards) are allowable:
    3.1. Localization

The "I Love U Guys" Foundation is committed to providing its programs at no cost to a widening variety of organizations.

To assess the fidelity of implementation within an organization, The Foundation has developed a certification program for the Standard Reunification Method (SRM). The certification program is optional and is not required to use the SRM within your organization.

## COPYRIGHTS AND TRADEMARKS

In order to protect the integrity and consistency of the Standard Reunification Method, The "I Love U Guys" Foundation exercises all protection under copyright and trademark. Use of this material is governed by the Terms of Use.

## WARNINGS AND DISCLAIMER

Every effort has been made to make this book as complete and accurate as possible, but no warranty or fitness is implied. The information provided is on an "as is" basis.

## AUTHOR/CONTRIBUTOR INFORMATION

John-Michael Keyes - Primary Author
The "I Love U Guys" Foundation
Executive Director

Russell Deffner - Contributing Author
The "I Love U Guys" Foundation
Advisor/Contractor/Volunteer

## SPECIAL THANKS

Pat Hamilton – Executive Director of Operations, Adams 12 Five Star Schools, Colorado

Jeff Genger – Director of Emergency Management, Adams 12 Five Star Schools, Colorado

John McDonald – Executive Director, Safety, Security and Emergency Planning, Jefferson County Public Schools, Colorado

Will Schwall – Emergency Manager, Hays County Sheriff's Office, San Marcos, Texas

Michelle Brady – Emergency Planning Coordinator, Hillsboro School District, Oregon

Heidi Walts – Sergeant, Broomfield Police, Colorado

## SRM REVIEW COMMITTEE

Pat Hamilton – Executive Director of Operations, Adams 12 Five Star Schools, Adams County, Colorado

Kevin Burd – Lieutenant, Hunterdon County Prosecutor's Office, New Jersey

Joseph Majsak – Senior Vice President & Chief Marketing Officer, Genesis Management & Insurance Services Corporation, Stamford, Connecticut

Kevin Griger – Captain, Sarpy County Sheriff's Office, Nebraska

## CONTACT INFORMATION

The "I Love U Guys" Foundation can be reached online at http://iloveuguys.org.

Email: srm@iloveuguys.org.

The "I Love U Guys" Foundation
PO Box 919
Conifer, CO 80433
303.426.3100

# "Recovery starts when the crisis begins."

**"Reunification is the first step in the recovery process."**
*– John McDonald, Executive Director of Safety and Emergency Planning, Jeffco R1, Colorado*

# STANDARD™ REUNIFICATION METHOD

## ABOUT THIS BOOK

In 2012, The "I Love U Guys" Foundation introduced the Standard Reunification Method. At the time, we saw a void in school safety planning regarding student/parent reunification after a crisis. We were certain this was a true need, but few schools or districts actually had reunification plans and practices in place. Fewer still had actually drilled or practiced.

Was it truly a need? The answer lies in the widespread adoption of the SRM. Since 2012, thousands of schools in the US and Canada have implemented the Standard Reunification Method as a means to safely reunite students and families after a crisis.

Recovery starts when the crisis begins. Reunification is the first step in that recovery.

This is Version 2.0 of the Standard Reunification Method. But notice, we use the word *method*. Not *protocol*. Not *procedure*. Method.

What that means is that we provide you with some tactics. Things we know. But the event, your reunification site, your environment, will ultimately dictate what you do.

Please, in your planning, if you see something here that doesn't seem to work in your environment, figure out what does. Let us know.

# "Cops own the crime. Fire owns the flames. Schools own the kids."

**"But Paramedics own the patient."**
*And that may be an area of conflict during an event.*
*Your reunification plan and methods must be*
*communicated with first responders prior to a crisis.*

## REUNIFICATION

The nation has experienced high profile acts of school violence. In response to this and the everyday types of crisis, The "I Love U Guys" Foundation develops programs to help districts, departments and agencies respond to incidents.

One critical aspect of crisis response is accountable reunification of students with their parents or guardians in the event a controlled release is necessary. The Standard Re-

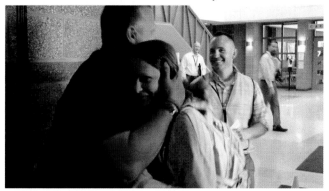

unification Method provides school and district safety teams proven methods for planning, practicing and achieving a successful reunification. Keep in mind though, this is an evolving process. While there is a smattering of science in these methods, there is certainly more art. Site-specific considerations will impact how these practices can be integrated into school and district safety plans. Successful planning and implementation will also demand partnerships with all responding agencies participating in a crisis response.

## WHY BOTHER?

Crisis recovery starts with the crisis, not after. Simply "winging it" when reuniting ignores not only the mental health demands that accompany a crisis, but the responsibility of the school and the district to maintain the chain of custody for every student.

No school is immune to stuff hitting the proverbial fan. Wildland or structural fires, hazardous materials, floods, tornados, blizzards, power outages, tsunamis, bomb threats, acts of violence, acts of terror... these just start the list of events that may necessitate a controlled reunification and release for a school or district.

A predetermined, practiced reunification method ensures the reunification process will not further complicate what is probably already a chaotic, anxiety-filled scene. In fact, putting an orderly reunification plan into action will help defuse emotion escalating at the site.

There is a hidden side effect of implementing the Standard Reunification Method. Going through the planning and training process may help strengthen district relationships with first responders. Often law enforcement is very active in partnering with schools and districts. Less often is the fire department. The SRM may be a vector into strengthening relationships with fire agencies as well.

## WHAT DOES IT COST?

Implementing the Standard Reunification Method concepts and planning stages take a certain amount of time. But in the grand scheme of school safety, the level of effort is modest. There will be some staff hours committed to the planning, training and practice of these concepts. There will be some cost in printing and in creating the "go kits" necessary for a successful reunification. Since some of this activity is happening at the district level, the cost of "go kits" can be spread among all of the schools in the district.

## ADAMS 12, FIVE STAR SCHOOLS METHOD

The core concept of the Adams 12 Reunification Method rests on accountability achieved through a process based on managing the physical location of students, staff and of incoming parents. The process also uses perforated cards. These cards are completed by parents or guardians at the reunification site. The cards are separated at the perforation, and a reunifier retrieves the child.

The methods detailed in the first version of the Standard Reunification Method are based on the practices developed at the Adams 12, Five Star School District, Thornton, Colorado, by Pat Hamilton, Executive Director of Operations, and also at Jefferson County School District, Golden, Colorado, by John McDonald, Executive Director of Security and Emergency Planning.

Since its introduction in 2012, other districts and agencies have also contributed.

The Job Action Sheets in this book were inspired by the work of Michelle Brady, Emergency Planning Coordinator, Hillsboro School District, Hillsboro, Oregon.

Other aspects of the Job Action Sheets in this book were inspired by the work of Kevin Sutherland, Emergency Planning Coordinator, Beaverton School District, Beaverton, Oregon.

Other materials were sourced from the phenomenal work of Will Schwall, Emergency Manager, Hays County Sheriff's Office, San Marcos, Texas.

## OBJECTIVES

The objective of this manual is to help districts develop, train and mobilize a district reunification team, and implement tangible, on-site and off-site reunification plans. Inherent in this objective is creating or strengthening partnerships with first responder agencies – police, fire and medical. By having district and school personnel build a well designed draft plan, it becomes easier to engage the first responders and other key participants in the planning process. During this process, a core philosophy is essential:

*Cops own the crime.*
*Fire owns the flames.*
*Schools own the kids.*
*Paramedics own the patient.*

Additionally, performing a successful reunification is much more likely when drills are conducted in advance of an incident. Tabletop exercises and live exercises should be scheduled and performed.

## THE PROCESS IN A NUTSHELL

The materials in this manual provide the fundamentals for a comprehensive district plan. The beauty of the Standard Reunification Method is its simplicity.

- Establish a parent check-in location.
- Deliver the students to the student staging area, beyond the field of vision of parents/guardians.
- Once students are on site, notify parents of location.
- "Greeters" direct parents/guardians to the parent check-in location, and help them understand the process.
- Parents/guardians complete Reunification Cards.
- Procedure allows parents/guardians to self-sort during check in, streamlining the process.
- The "Reunifier" recovers student from the student staging area and delivers to the parent.
- Controlled lines of sight allow for an orderly flow, and issues can be handled with diminished drama or anxiety.
- Medical, notification, or investigative contingencies are anticipated.
- Pedestrian "flows" are created so lines don't cross.
- When it's all said and done, successful reunification is about managing the student/parent experience.

## WHEN TO INITIATE A REUNIFICATION

Initiating a reunification can be a result of anything abnormal at the school or in the area: power or phone outage, weather event, hazmat incident, bomb threats, criminal activity in the area, or active violence at the school.

In some cases it may be only a partial student population reunification. For instance, criminal activity in the area might result in reunifying students who walk to and from school.

## KEEP PARENTS OUTSIDE

The process works best when you can keep the parents outside of the building. If weather or circumstance dictate parents should be inside the building, give special attention to walking flows and sightlines. Caution tape is a secret "force field" when establishing the parent staging areas within a building.

## WHY USE CARDS?

Many schools use electronic rosters or campus information systems. Wouldn't that be easier? The reality is a little different. First and foremost is access to data. Foundation research indicates that in any high profile incident, and even many local ones, internet and cell service become intermittent or even unresponsive. Often school WiFi is impacted as well.

## THE CARD

The Reunification Card does a ton of work. Its primary function is to provide accountability, so one student per card is recommended. It also helps with the parent experience. The card is perforated and gives parents a sense of progress as they go through the process.

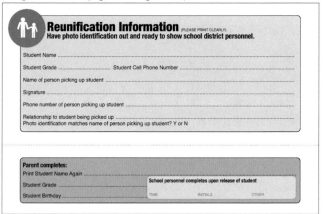

## A LITTLE SOCIAL ENGINEERING

A reunification typically occurs because of a crisis or emergency. Consequently, not just students and parents are trying to function at extraordinary stress levels; staff, their families and other first responders also feel the strain. By having a defined process with signage, cards, branding, procedures and protocols, the school presents an organized, calm face to all involved. Fear or uncertainty often results from the unknown. By adopting, communicating and practicing a "known" procedure, the school removes some of that uncertainty.

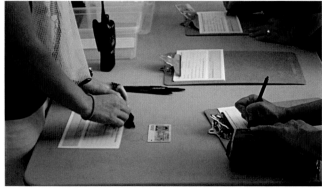

The cards also bring anxiety down a notch. Asking a parent to complete the form is a familiar activity and will demand the parent slow down and perform a cognitive action, "Here, read the instructions on back, and we'll get things started," might be the first step in lowering parental blood pressure.

## INCIDENT COMMAND SYSTEM

Whether it is a man-made or natural crisis, or an act of violence in the school, law enforcement, fire and medical teams will be involved in the school or district's reunification process. Learning to understand and speak a common language as well as being familiar with their procedures is imperative to a successful outcome. With that in mind, district and school safety teams must understand and use the Incident Command System.

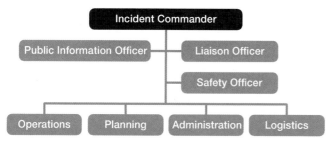

## NOT SO WEIRD ADVICE

At first blush, this bit of advice may sound weird to educators: *"Check out FEMA. Go to http://training.fema.gov and complete the online training for IS-100 SCa Introduction to Incident Management for Schools."* The course takes about an hour and a half to complete and introduces some basic emergency response principles in the context of school safety.

Here's why this advice isn't as weird as it sounds. Every first responder agency that partners with schools uses "Incident Command" during a crisis. The "Incident Command System" (ICS) is a response method that determines the role of everyone responding to a crisis and defines a shared vocabulary and shared expectations of behavior.

District and school safety teams need this shared vocabulary when interacting with first responders during a crisis. Equally important is that, when meeting with first responders, having the concepts and vocabulary of Incident Command removes some of the language barriers. It also shows a commitment to success that departments and agencies will appreciate.

## PRIORITY, OBJECTIVE, STRATEGY, TACTIC

A valuable FEMA resource is the *Incident Action Planning Guide,* and it's a good start in understanding how first responders manage an incident.

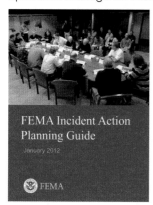

From a school or district perspective, it's important to understand that the incident commander has an expectation that to be useful during the event, the school or district personnel need to have some experience with incident command.

If the school or district personnel don't exhibit any knowledge of the process, their input may be marginalized.

**Source:** *https://www.fema.gov/media-library/assets/documents/25028*

## ARTICULATE YOUR P.O.S.T.

The first step in incident management is defining the priorities, objectives, strategies and tactics that will be used during the event. While every incident will be unique, there are considerations that can be addressed in advance.

**Priorities:**
- Student and staff safety and well being.
- Student and staff whereabouts and condition.
- Starting the recovery process.

**Objectives:**
- Every student has been accounted for.
- Every staff member has been accounted for.
- Every student still in the school's control is reunited with their parent or guardian.

**Strategies:**
- The Standard Reunification Method

**Tactics:**
- Tactics will vary based on the event and the environment, but look at the typical lifecycles on page 16 for a jumpstart.

## JOINT INFORMATION CENTER AND THE SOCIAL MEDIA TEAM

An essential role in the JIC is the Social Media Team. The team should have a couple of people monitoring social media outlets, and when directed by the lead Public Information Officer, releasing any information to social media outlets. Twitter especially seems to have the highest level of activity during an event.

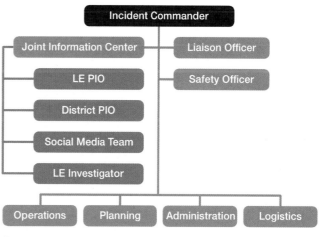

If possible, Public Information Officers (PIO) from all of the responding departments or agencies and the district PIO should be physically together with the Social Media Team. If it's a criminal event, there is a growing trend for law enforcement to assign a detective or investigator to the JIC to monitor social media for evidentiary information.

It is important to recognize that if students have been transported to a separate reunification site, a second command structure will be set up there as well. It may be labeled as a division under Unified Command and will need resources from first responders, but a command structure will need to be established to manage the reunification process, separate from the initial incident.

## TWO TEAMS:
## TRANSPORT AND REUNIFICATION

With an offsite reunification, the district reunification team will deploy to the reunification site. Other responsibilities need to be managed at the impacted school. Regardless of criminal activity, law enforcement resources will be required.

There are two teams the district must field for an offsite reunification. The team at the impacted school facilitates transport and initiates accountability processing.

The reunification team deploys to the reunification site for staging and ultimately student/parent reunification, and return transportation of teachers and staff.

## IMPACTED SCHOOL: TRANSPORT TEAM

The team at the impacted school has these priorities:

- Assemble a master student roster, teacher roster and guest roster
- Identify and notify reunification site
- Provide safe transport of students and staff to reunification site
- If there are injuries, additional district personnel assign to the receiving care facilities.

## LAW ENFORCEMENT SUPPORT

At the impacted site law enforcement support may be necessary. Some assignments may include:

- Traffic Control
- Crowd Control
- ID Verification
- Perimeter Control
- Security
- Liaison

In the event of criminal activity, LE will typically take the lead in Unified Command.

At the secure assembly area, law enforcement may search students and staff. One important consideration for law enforcement is, if possible, perform the search of students out of sight of the media.

## TRANSPORTATION DIRECTOR

Whether the district runs its own buses or service is contracted out, the Transportation Director should be involved in all planning, drilling and training for reunification.

## TRANSPORT OPERATIONAL
## ROLES AND DUTIES

The following outlines the roles and duties of the Transportation Team. For detailed tasks see the Job Action Sheets.

**Transport Incident Commander** Coordinate Priorities, Objectives, Strategies and Tactics for an accountable, easy, reunification of students with parents.

**Public Information Officer** Communicate with parents and press, if appropriate. Coordinate use of mass call or text messages

**Social Media Team** Monitor social media. Use Twitter to communicate with parents and press, if appropriate.

**Safety Officer** Observe site and remedy safety concerns.

**Liaison Officer** Communicate with Fire, Medical or Law Enforcement.

**Operations Chief** Establish and manage operational staff.

**Planning Chief** Establish and manage planning staff.

**Finance/Administration Chief** Establish and manage administrative staff.

**Logistics Chief** Establish and manage logistical staff.

**Student Assembly Director** Establish and manage the Student Assembly Area.

**Leads** For span of control, some roles may need leads.

**Victim Advocates/Counselors** Standby unless needed.

**Kid Wranglers** Teachers and Staff who arrive with students remain in the Student Assembly Area to manage students. Additional people may be assigned to this task.

**Scribe** Document events. A yellow pad is sufficient.

**Runner** Assist Incident Command if needed.

**Transportation** Direct transportation needs.

**Communications** Facilitate radio and other communication needs.

**Facilities** Coordinate any physical plant needs.

**School Principal** High priority for transport to the reunification site. Be present at Parent reunification site.

**Superintendent** Verify reunification site and notification.

## TEACHERS: STAY WITH YOUR STUDENTS

Interviews with safety directors directly impacted by crisis reveal a common thread. Often teachers will group together in the immediate aftermath, or assume their job is done when police arrive on scene. It's important to emphasize that teachers should remain with their students and aren't done until all of the students have been reunited with their families. Certainly, exceptions are appropriate for teachers who are also parents of impacted students.

# SAMPLE TRANSPORT ORGANIZATION CHART

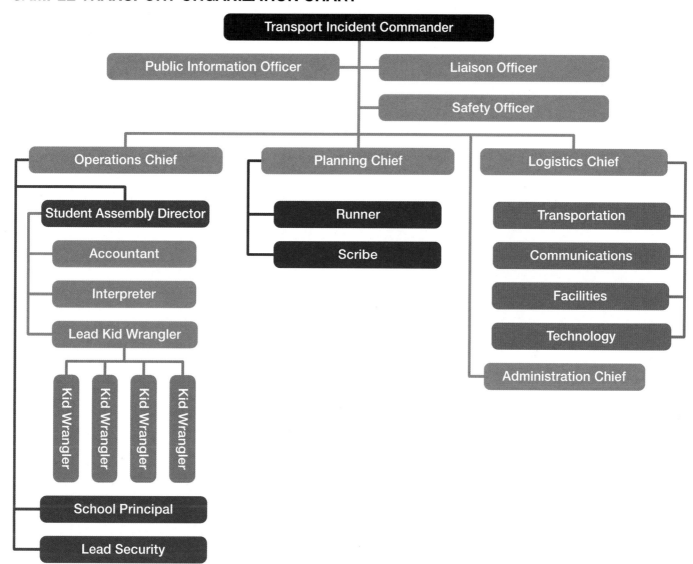

## THE DISTRICT REUNIFICATION TEAM

Most often the Reunification Team is populated by district personnel. There are several reasons for this:

- Training can be more readily coordinated.
- Experienced teams are more proficient.
- School based teams may initially be unavailable.

Smaller districts may recruit from various schools' administrators in order to populate the team. Extremely small districts may recruit volunteers from the community to staff the Reunification Team. A good rule of thumb for team size is one per hundred students, plus another five members.

Once school staff are at the reunification site, there are roles that the school staff will assume. It's important to train school staff in their role during a reunification.

## WHO ARE VICTIM ADVOCATES?

Many law enforcement agencies, district attorneys, and prosecutors have victim advocates on staff and a cadre of volunteers. They often deploy when there is a crisis. Very often they are trained in Psychological First Aid and can be helpful with crisis counseling, if needed, during a reunification. Recruit and train these community partners.

## INCLUDING FIRST RESPONDERS

It is absolutely imperative that as the reunification plan is developed, first responders are brought into the process. Meeting with command staff, including PIOs, both law enforcement and Fire/EMS will generate two outcomes. First, they will look at your plan from their perspective. Second, they have suggestions you might not have thought of.

During a Standard Reunification Method workshop, conducted by The Foundation, a fire chief requested the training for every fire station in his city. When questioned why, he replied, "We are going to be on scene. If we're not actively engaged in fire or EMS, we can help with the reunification process."

## LAW ENFORCEMENT SUPPORT

At the reunification site law enforcement support may be necessary. Some assignments may include:

- Traffic Control
- Crowd Control
- ID Verification
- Perimeter Control
- Security
- Liaison

## OPERATIONAL ROLES AND DUTIES

The following outlines the roles and duties of the Reunification Team. For detailed tasks see the Job Action Sheets.

**Reunification Incident Commander** Coordinate Priorities, Objectives, Strategies and Tactics for an accountable, easy reunification of students with parents.

**Public Information Officer** Communicate with parents and press, if appropriate. Coordinate use of mass call or text messages.

**Social Media Team** Monitor social media. Tweet parents and press, if appropriate.

**Safety Officer** Observe site and remedy safety concerns.

**Liaison Officer** Communicate with Fire, Medical or Law Enforcement.

**Operations Chief** Establish and manage operational staff.

**Planning Chief** Establish and manage planning staff.

**Finance/Administration Chief** Establish and manage administrative staff.

**Logistics Chief** Establish and manage logistical staff.

**Parent Check-in Director** Establish and manage the check-in process.

**Student Assembly Director** Establish and manage the Student Assembly Area.

**Leads** For span of control, some roles may need leads.

**Greeters** Help coordinate the parent lines. Tell parents about the process. Help verify parents without ID.

**Checkers** Verify ID and possibly custody rights of parents or guardians. Direct parents to Reunification Area.

**Reunifier** Take bottom of Reunification Card to Assembly Area, locate student and bring to Reunification Area. Ask student, "Are you okay going home with this person?"

**Flow Monitor** Observe and remedy process hiccups.

**Victim Advocates/Counselors** Standby unless needed.

**Kid Wranglers** Teachers and Staff who arrive with students remain in the Student Assembly Area to manage students. Additional people may be assigned to this task.

**Entertainment Director** At the elementary level, deploying a projector and screen can reduce student stress. With middle and high school students, consider turning on a television and tuning to local news if appropriate.

**Scribe** Document events. A yellow pad is sufficient.

**Runner** Assist Incident Command if needed.

**Transportation** Directs transportation needs.

**Nutrition Services** Provide snacks and water.

**Communications** Facilitate radio and other communication needs.

**Facilities** Coordinate any physical plant needs.

**School Principal** Serve as the "Face of the school" at the Reunification Area.

# SAMPLE OFFSITE REUNIFICATION ORGANIZATION CHART

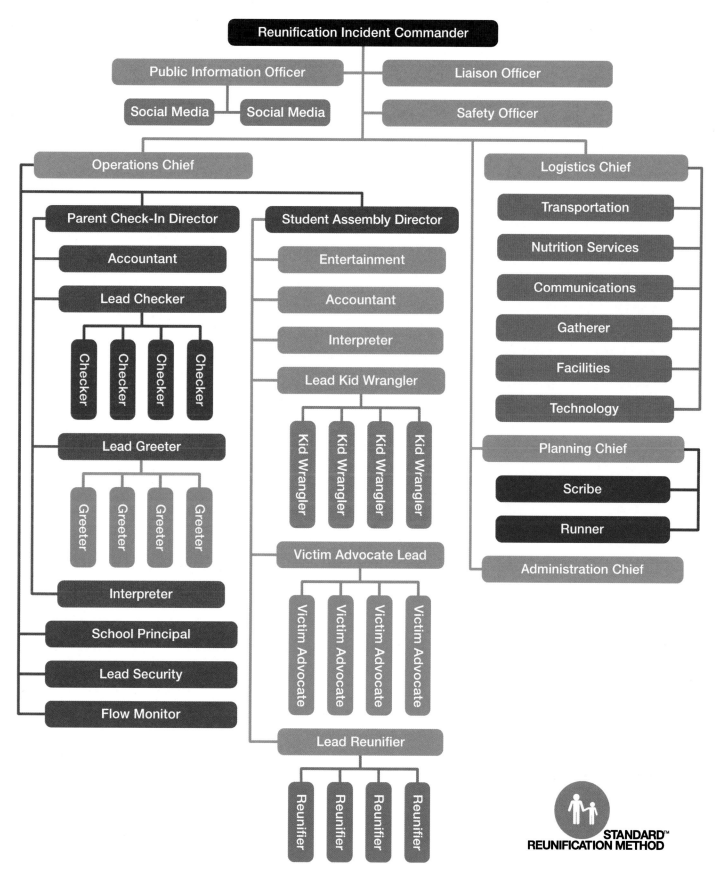

# SRP Lifecycle with

## EXAMPLE 1: SECURE (LOCKOUT)

**Scenario:** Criminal activity in the area has resulted in the school going into a Secure (Lockout) condition. Students were brought into the building. Business as usual inside, but no one is let in or out.

Law enforcement has indicated that a normal release of the students can occur, but the situation outside isn't resolved.

**Considerations:** With criminal activity in area of the school, it's decided that students who walk home should have their parents pick them up.

**Reunification Incident Command:** Because there was no criminal or safety issue in the school, Reunification Incident Command would be led by the school safety team. Coordination with Law Enforcement Incident Command of the criminal activity would be needed.

**Public Information Officer:** Because the school was not directly involved in criminal activity, the school or district would lead public information within the school community. District PIO would inform LE PIO of the media messaging.

**Notifications:** Depending on the situation, parents and media may be notified that the school has been placed in Secure (Lockout). Additional notification will be made to parents who would need to pick up their students.

**Police Role in Reunification:** With criminal activity in the area, but not directly near the school, officers may be asked to assist with reunification. Some duties might include assisting with parent identification (for the parents without ID), traffic control, or simply uniformed presence. Patrol resources may also be relocated near the school.

## SECURE LIFECYCLE
- School is placed in a Secure (Lockout) condition.
- Parents are notified.
- Business goes as usual within the school.
- Law enforcement presence around the school is increased
- The Standard Reunification Method is utilized for the students that walk home at the end of school day.

## EXAMPLE 2: LOCKDOWN

**Scenario**: At the middle school, an armed intruder is seen in the building. Students and staff lock classroom doors, turn out the lights, and remain out of sight. Law enforcement arrives on scene.

**Considerations**: Because it is still an active law enforcement response and investigation, the decision is made to transport the students to a nearby community center for reunification.

**Unified Command**: Because it is an active crime scene, law enforcement would lead Unified Command at the middle school site.

**Reunification Incident Command**: At the reunification site, a command structure is established to manage the reunification.

**Joint Information Center**: Because it is an active crime scene, the law enforcement PIO would be the primary press representative. The school or district PIO would be in the JIC, communicating with the PIO at the reunification site.

**Notifications**: Parents and media are notified that the school has been placed in Lockdown. Additional notifications are made to parents on the location of the reunification site once students are in route or at the site.

**Police Role in Reunification**: While the school has become an active crime scene, some officers will be assigned to the reunification site. Depending on the site, police may decide to sweep the area prior to students arriving. In addition to the duties outlined in the Lockout example, detectives may be on scene for witness interviews and statements.

## LOCKDOWN LIFECYCLE
- School is placed in Lockdown.
- Multiple law enforcement agencies arrive on scene.
- Students and staff are evacuated classroom by classroom to the Secure Assembly Area. In this case, the gym is secured by law enforcement.
- Parents begin to arrive outside of the police perimeter.
- The media arrive on scene.
- Internet, WiFi, and cell services become intermittent or unresponsive.
- Police secure the reunification site.
- District mobilizes Reunification Team.
- Buses are deployed and students are transported to the reunification site.
- Parents are notified of location.
- The Standard Reunification Method is utilized.

# Reunification

## EXAMPLE 3: EVACUATE

**Scenario:** An unknown cause has resulted in thick smoke in the middle school. Students successfully evacuate to the football field.

**Considerations:** Because it is still an active fire response and investigation, the decision is made to transport the students to a nearby high school for reunification.

**Unified Command:** Because it is an active fire event, the fire department would lead Unified Command at the middle school site.

**Reunification Incident Command:** At the reunification site, a command structure is established to manage the reunification.

**Joint Information Center:** Because it is an active fire event, the fire department PIO would be the primary press representative. The school or district PIO would be in the JIC, communicating with the PIO at the reunification site.

**Notifications:** Parents and media are notified that the school has been evacuated. Additional notifications are made to parents on the location of the reunification site once students are in route or at the site.

**Police Role in Reunification:** While the school is an active fire scene, the school requests assistance from law enforcement. Officers are assigned to the reunification site.

## EVACUATE LIFECYCLE
- Parents begin to arrive outside of the perimeter.
- The media arrive on scene.
- Internet, WiFi, and cell services are intermittent or unresponsive.
- Police secure the reunification site.
- District mobilizes Reunification Team.
- Buses are deployed and students are transported to the reunification site.
- Parents are notified of site location.
- The Standard Reunification Method is utilized.

## EXAMPLE 4: SHELTER

**Scenario:** A nearby wildland fire has resulted in mandatory neighborhood evacuations. The Red Cross is requesting the high school as a designated shelter.

**Considerations:** Due to the community value of the high school as a Red Cross shelter, the decision is made to accept the request. With area residents arriving, and bus routes affected, the decision is made to transport students to a school outside of the impacted area.

**Unified Command:** Because it is an active fire event, the fire department would lead Unified Command, but shelter is only one aspect. The Red Cross would establish their command structure division at the shelter high school.

**Reunification Incident Command:** At the reunification site, a command structure is established to manage the reunification.

**Joint Information Center:** Because it is a large scale event, managed by Unified Command, the most experienced PIO would be the primary press representative. The school or district PIO would be in the JIC, communicating with the PIO at the reunification site.

**Notifications:** Parents and media are notified that the school has been evacuated. Additional notifications are made to parents on the location of the reunification site once students are in route or at the site.

**Police Role in Reunification:** The school which is the reunification site requests assistance from law enforcement. Officers are assigned to the reunification site.

## SHELTER LIFECYCLE
- Parents begin to arrive outside of the perimeter.
- The media arrive on scene.
- Internet, WiFi, and cell services are intermittent or unresponsive.
- Police secure the reunification site.
- District mobilizes Reunification Team.
- Buses are deployed and students are transported to the reunification site.
- Parents are notified of site location.
- The Standard Reunification Method is utilized.

# SRM Staging the

## STEP 1
### ESTABLISH ONSITE INCIDENT COMMAND

The first step in staging for transport is establishing School Incident Command at the affected school. Integrating with Unified Command should be a priority.

**Priorities:** Student and staff safety and wellbeing
Student and staff whereabouts and condition
Assemble affected school command staff
Integrate with Unified Command
Joint Information Center established

**Objectives:** Safe transport of students and staff to reunification site

**Strategy:** The Standard Reunification Method

**Tactics:** Will be determined by the environment

## STEP 2
### CLASSROOM EVACUATION

Classrooms are individually evacuated to the Secure Assembly Area. During a Police Led Evacuation, students and staff will be asked to keep their hands visible.

If it is a Police Led Evacuation after a Lockdown, each room will be cleared by Law Enforcement personnel. This process may take up to several hours. Teacher should take attendance in the classroom, prior to evacuation.

### SPECIAL NEEDS POPULATIONS

If there is a diverse special needs population, consider evacuating that population last. Once evacuated, this population will demand additional resources.

# SRM Actions and

## COMMUNITY ACTION
### PARENTS WILL BEGIN TO ARRIVE

Parents will be arriving at the impacted school. Often with a Lockdown event, adjoining schools will go into Lockout. Parents may be arriving at those schools as well.

## REUNIFICATION SITE
### MOBILIZE REUNIFICATION TEAM

Contacting the Superintendent and determining the Reunification Site are among the first actions taken. If the site is another school, early release may be necessary.

# School for Transport

## STEP 3
### SECURE ASSEMBLY AREA

At the Secure Assembly Area it is preferable that teachers stay with their students. If some teachers are unable to be at the Secure Assembly Area, doubling up classes with "Partner" teachers is appropriate.

## STEP 4
### STUDENT AND STAFF TRANSPORT

Students and staff board the bus and are transported to the Reunification Site. Buses having audio video systems can be utilized for further accountability by having students face the camera and state their name.

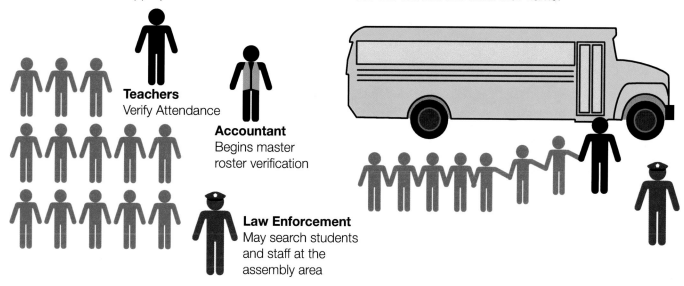

**Teachers**
Verify Attendance

**Accountant**
Begins master roster verification

**Law Enforcement**
May search students and staff at the assembly area

# Considerations

## LAW ENFORCEMENT
### SUPPORT AND INVESTIGATIONS

Regardless of criminal activity, law enforcement support will be necessary at both the impacted school and the reunification site.

## FIRE AND EMS
### CASUALTY CARE

If necessary, Fire and EMS will establish Casualty Collection, Triage and Transport areas. Many fire departments are also willing to assist in the transport and reunification process, if they are not actively responding to crisis.

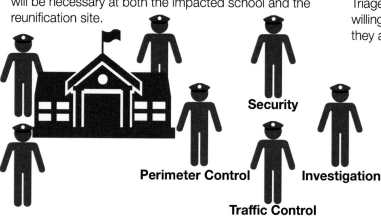

**Security**

**Perimeter Control**

**Investigation**

**Traffic Control**

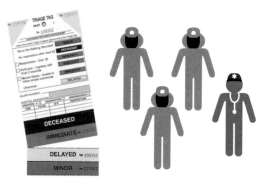

# SRM Staging the

## ASSEMBLY AREA
### STUDENTS ENTER OUT OF PARENTAL VIEW

Students are transported to the Reunification Site and are then directed to the Student Assembly Area. Often this is a cafeteria or gymnasium. Upon arrival, students are verified against a master roster.

It is important that students are not in view of their parents when exiting the bus and entering the reunification site.

**Law Enforcement**
Often an Officer is posted where students are disembarking.

LE

**Transport Students to Site**

## GREETING AREA
### PARENTS ARE MET HERE

As parents arrive, signage directs them to Parent Check-in Table. Greeters begin the process by asking parents to complete the Reunification Card.

**Student Check-in Table**

**Law Enforcement Interviews**

**Student Assembly Area**

**Helpful Tip**
As parents wait for reunification with their student, try to have them clustered rather than in a line. Students may not always be recovered in the order parents line up.

**Law Enforcement**
Often an Officer is posted where parents wait for reunification.

LE

**Parent Reunification Area**

# Reunification Site

## CHECK-IN TABLE
### SET UP MULTIPLE LINES
Establish parallel check-in lines based on first initial of last name. Checkers verify ID and custody.

## REUNIFICATION AREA
### PARENT STUDENT REUNIFICATION
As their tasks are completed, Greeters and Checkers can be reassigned as Reunifiers.

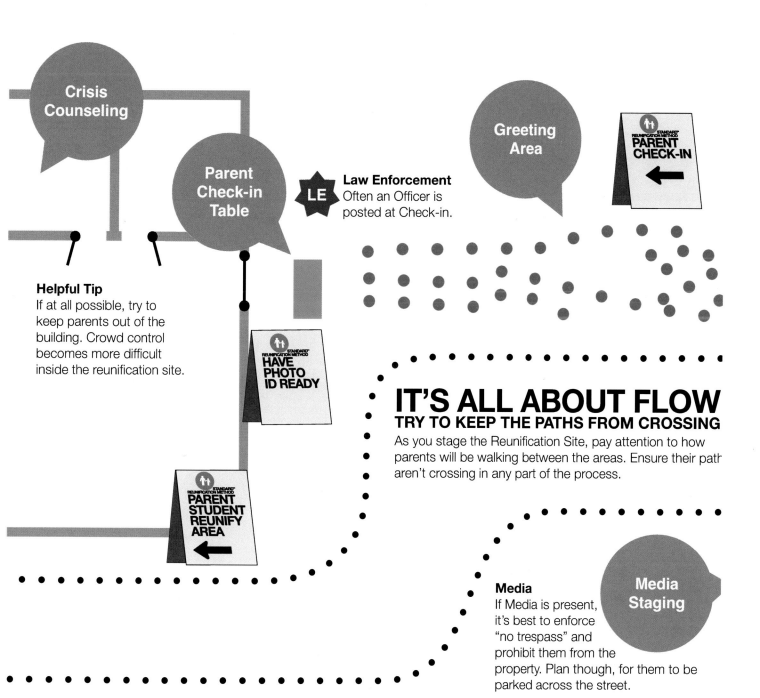

**Crisis Counseling**

**Parent Check-in Table**

**LE** **Law Enforcement** Often an Officer is posted at Check-in.

**Greeting Area**

**PARENT CHECK-IN** ←

**Helpful Tip**
If at all possible, try to keep parents out of the building. Crowd control becomes more difficult inside the reunification site.

**HAVE PHOTO ID READY**

**PARENT STUDENT REUNIFY AREA** ←

## IT'S ALL ABOUT FLOW
### TRY TO KEEP THE PATHS FROM CROSSING
As you stage the Reunification Site, pay attention to how parents will be walking between the areas. Ensure their path aren't crossing in any part of the process.

**Media**
If Media is present, it's best to enforce "no trespass" and prohibit them from the property. Plan though, for them to be parked across the street.

**Media Staging**

# SRM The Process

## STEP 1
### GREETINGS
As parents arrive at the reunification site, Greeters explain the process and distribute Reunification Cards.

## STEP 2
### PARENTS FILL OUT CARD
Parents complete the information requested on the card, and begin to self-sort into lines.

## STEP 3
### CHECKERS VERIFY ID
Parent custody is verified. The card is torn on the perforation and the bottom is returned to the parent. The top is given to the Accountant.

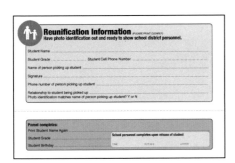

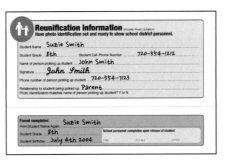

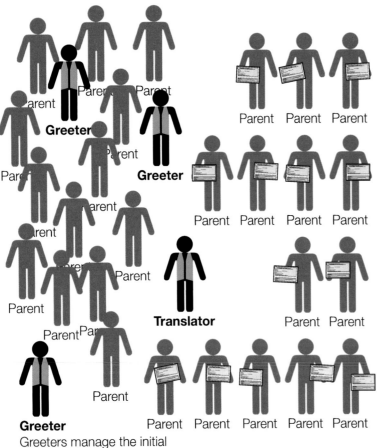

**Greeter**
Greeters manage the initial intake of parents, explaining the process and answering questions that may arise.

**ABC** — Checker

**DEFGHIJK** — Checker

**LMN** — Checker

**OPQ..XYZ** — Checker

Checkers verify identification. In some cases custodial authority may need verification as well.

**Accountant**
The Accountant verifies cards against a master roster and may start sorting cards.

**Law Enforcement**
A uniformed officer can help with crowd control and identity verification.

# in 6 Easy Steps

## STEP 4
### REUNIFICATION AREA

At the Reunification Area, parents give the bottom of the card to a Reunifier. The Reunifier goes to the Assembly area to get the student.

## STEP 5
### STUDENT REUNIFICATION

The Reunifier returns the student to their parents asking the student if they feel comfortable leaving with that adult. They then note the time and initial the bottom of the card.

## STEP 6
### ACCOUNTABILITY

The Reunifier delivers the bottom of the card to the Student Assembly Accountant. The Accountant may start sorting the cards.

Parent  Parent  Parent  **Reunifier** ● ● ● **Reunifier** ● ● ● **Reunifier**    Parent ● ● ● **Reunifier Accountant**

**Principal**

It may be beneficial to have the school principal in the area where students and parents are reunified.

## WHAT IF?
### THE STUDENT ISN'T THERE

If the student isn't in the Assembly Area, the Reunifier hands the card to a Victim Advocate/Crisis Counselor.

## SEPARATE
### PARENT FROM THE LINE

The Victim Advocate/Crisis Counselor then separates the parent from the other parents in line and takes them to a private location.

**Law Enforcement**

A uniformed officer can help with crowd control and keep the peace.

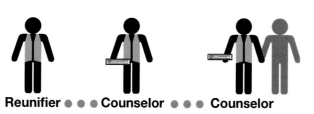

**Reunifier** ● ● ● **Counselor** ● ● ● **Counselor**

Parent  Parent  Parent  Parent

# SRM The Card

## REUNIFICATION INFORMATION CARDS

The Standard Reunification Method was created to manage not just the students, but the parental experience of reunification as well. The Reunification Card is an essential element of the method.

Some might initially protest, "What! More Paperwork?" And the answer is "Yes. Precisely." Beyond providing a mechanism for accountability, the card demonstrates to parents that there is a process for this. It shows that school or district has a plan and a method.

The psychology behind the process begins to offer the parent some measure of order in what might be a stressful time. Filling the card out, then separating the top from the bottom, handing the card to the Reunifier, gives the parent feedback, demonstrating progress in the process. The bottom of the card also provides proxy identification for the parent, removing the need to ID them at every phase.

## SEND IT HOME IN ADVANCE?

The question often comes up on whether the school should send the cards home in advance and request parents fill out and return them. Certainly an option, but it creates unnecessary work in collecting the cards and diminishes the parent experience. One alternative is to send the cards home, with the handout, and ask parents to complete the card and put it in their car. This gives parents an expectation of the process and some parents will complete the request. The handout is available on the website and is also reprinted on page 28 of this book.

## AVAILABLE IN SPANISH

The Reunification Card is also available in Spanish. Check the website for new translations.

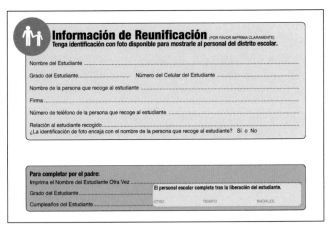

## PRESS READY ARTWORK

The Reunification Cards are press ready for your printer. The artwork is set up for *Work and Tumble*[1] on 8½" x 11" index card stock. Ask your printer for a strong perforation. There is little worse than a "bad perf" on reunification day.

[1] *"In prepress and printing, an imposition or layout in which one plate contains all the images (pages) to be printed on both sides of a sheet. When one side of a job has been printed, the pile of printed sheets is turned over, the edge of the sheet that was the gripper edge for the first side becoming the back edge for the second side. After printing, the sheet is cut in half, yielding two identical units."*

**Source:** *PrintWiki – the Free Encyclopedia of Print. http://printwiki.org*

# Reunification Information (PLEASE PRINT CLEARLY)
## Have photo identification out and ready to show school district personnel.

Student Name ...........................................................................................................................................

Student Grade ................................... Student Cell Phone Number ...............................................................

Name of person picking up student .........................................................................................................

Signature ................................................................................................................................................

Phone number of person picking up student .............................................................................................

Relationship to student being picked up ....................................................................................................
Photo identification matches name of person picking up student? Y or N

---

## Parent completes:

Print Student Name Again ........................................................................................................................

Student Grade ..............................................................

Student Birthday ..........................................................

### School personnel completes upon release of student

TIME                    INITIALS                    OTHER

---

## Parent Guardian Sign Off

I have read and understand these instructions.

Print Your Name ....................................................Date ............................

Signature ............................................................

---

## Reunification

First, we want to thank you for your patience during this reunification. We share the same goal during this process: Getting you and your student back together as quickly as possible. The reason we're going through this is that an event has occurred at the school that mandates we personally reunite you with your child.

### Instructions

1. Please complete the information on the other side of this card.
2. Prepare identification (If you don't have ID with you, please move to the side of the line, it may take a little longer to verify your identity.)
3. Select the check-in line based on either student last name or student grade.
4. After check-in, staff will split this card and a runner will be sent to recover your student. Please step over to the Reunification Location.
5. If there has been injury or other concerns, you may be asked to meet a counselor.
6. Please don't shout at school or district staff. We'll get through this as quickly as possible.

# STANDARD™ REUNIFICATION METHOD

## STUDENT/PARENT REUNIFICATION

Circumstances may occur at the school that require parents to pick up their students in a formalized, controlled release. This process is called a Reunification and may be necessary due to weather, a power outage, hazmat or if a crisis occurs at the school. The Standard Reunification Method is a protocol that makes this process more predictable and less chaotic for all involved.

Because a reunification is not a typical end of school day event, a reunification may occur at a different location than the school a student attends. If this location is another school, then those students may be subject to a controlled release as well.

## NOTIFICATION

Parents may be notified in a number of ways. The school or district may use its broadcast phone or text message system. In some cases, students may be asked to send a text message to their parents. A reunification text message from a student may look something like this: *"The school has closed, please pick me up at 3:25 at the main entrance. Bring your ID. "*

## PARENT/GUARDIAN EXPECTATIONS

If a parent or guardian is notified that a reunification is needed, there are some expectations that parents or guardians should be aware of. First, bring identification. That will streamline things during reunification. Second, be patient. Reunification is a process that protects both the safety of the student and provides for an accountable change of custody from the school to a recognized custodial parent or guardian.

## WHAT IF A PARENT CAN'T PICK-UP THEIR STUDENT?

When a parent can't immediately go to the reunification site, students will only be released to individuals previously identified as a student's emergency contact. Otherwise, the school will hold students until parents can pick up their student.

## WHAT IF THE STUDENT DROVE TO SCHOOL?

There may be instances where a student may not be allowed to remove a vehicle from the parking lot. In this case, parents are advised to recover the student. In some circumstances, high school students may be released on their own.

**Reunification Information** (PLEASE PRINT CLEARLY)
Have photo identification out and ready to show school district personnel.

Student Name ................................................................
Student Grade ........................... Student Cell Phone Number ...............
Name of person picking up student .....................................
Signature ..................................................................
Phone number of person picking up student .............................
Relationship to student being picked up ................................
Photo identification matches name of person picking up student? Y or N

Parent completes:
Print Student Name Again ...............................................
Student Grade ..........................
Student Birthday .......................

School personnel completes upon release of student
TIME          INITIALS          OTHER

## HOW IT WORKS

For students, the school asks that students be orderly and quiet while waiting. Students may be asked to text a message to their parents or guardians. Students are also asked not to send other text messages either in or out of the school or reunification area. Keeping the cellular network usage at a minimum may be important during a reunification.

## REUNIFICATION CARDS

For parents, there are a couple of steps. If a parent is driving to the school, greater awareness of traffic and emergency vehicles is advised. Parents should park where indicated and not abandon vehicles. Parents are asked to go to the Reunification "Check In" area and form lines based on the first letter of their student's last name. While in line, parents are asked to fill out a reunification card. This card is perforated and will be separated during the process. Some of the same information is repeated on both the top and separated bottom of the card. Parents are asked to complete all parts of the card.

In the case of multiple students being reunified, a separate card for each student needs to be completed.

## BRING ID TO CHECK IN

During check in, identification and custody rights are confirmed. The card is separated and the bottom half given back to the parent.

From the "Check In" area parents are directed to the "Reunification" area. There, a runner will take the bottom half of the card and take it to the Student Assembly Area to recover the student or students.

Parents should be aware that in some cases, they may be invited into the building for further information.

## INTERVIEWS AND COUNSELING

In some cases, parents may be advised that a law enforcement investigation is underway and may be advised that interviews are necessary. In extreme cases, parents may be pulled aside for emergency or medical information.

# SRM Signage

**READY TO PRINT SIGNAGE**
Available on the website are downloadable signs. These are sized at 24" x 32," comfortably fitting in most sandwich board curb frames.

# SRM Planning

## GETTING STARTED

Planning for a reunification involves creating documents geared toward a number of audiences. There is a District plan, individual school plans, and plans for first responders.

As with any school safety plan, the concept of plan evolution is ever-present. Events may occur or lessons may be learned that impact these roles or procedures. Emergency planners should also remain vigilant and familiarize themselves with emerging trends regarding school safety and crisis response management in particular.

Additionally, depending on the type of event, plans may suggest Districts ask law enforcement to help evaluate and secure evacuation locations prior to moving students.

## THE DISTRICT REUNIFICATION PLAN HAS THE FOLLOWING COMPONENTS:

- Introduction
- Objectives
- Planning team acknowledgment and contact information
- Definitions
- Contact information
- Incident Command structure
- Attendance procedures
- Local site floor plan
- Primary walking evacuation site floor plan
- Primary walking evacuation routes with emergency services routes
- Secondary walking evacuation site floor plan
- Secondary walking evacuation routes with emergency services routes
- Transport plan
- Primary bus evacuation site floor plan
- Primary bus evacuation routes
- School, district, law enforcement, fire, medical, legal and insurance acknowledgment sign-offs
- Emergency services routes
- Secondary bus evacuation site floor plan
- Secondary bus evacuation routes with emergency services routes
- (Optional tertiary bus site information)
- District/School "go kits"
- Notification procedures
- Media management
- Time of day contingencies
- Type of incident contingencies
- Reunification Setup roles and procedures
- Reunification Process roles and procedures
- Reunification Teardown roles and procedures
- Debriefing guidance
- Exercise schedule
- Special needs considerations
- Memoranda of Understanding

## FLOOR PLANS AND SITE MAPS

It's important to include on- and off-site floor plans in the reunification plan. If the off-site evacuation location is another school, it's usually a reciprocal case. Given that condition, advance communication and distributed effort can result in both schools having each other's floor plans.

There may be different versions of the floor plan for each reunification location.

- A floor plan with no annotation
- A floor plan annotating student locations during an on-site reunification
- A floor plan annotating both home and guest student locations during an off-site reunification. Occupancy limits should be noted on all rooms used during an off-site reunification.
- A floor plan annotating occupancy in the case of an off-site location not being a school
- A site map with traffic responsibilities
- A site map with the locations of students, check-in and reunification

In the event of criminal activity, witness interview rooms and crisis counselor rooms should be annotated.

In the event of law enforcement debriefing needs, it is strongly suggested that a separate facility be used. While it may initially appear expeditious to conduct law enforcement or SWAT debriefings at the reunification location, further consideration may reveal that recovery of all participants may be impacted by co-mingling first responders and civilians.

## EVACUATION ROUTES

In mapping both walking and bus evacuation routes, it's important to identify potential traffic issues and first responder ingress and egress paths. The routes from the nearest fire station and the routes to the nearest hospitals must be considered. Are walking paths crossing streets that will be used by first responders? Are there some predictable streets that would be common for parents to use?

## SEXUAL OFFENDERS

It is also beneficial to determine the nature of the neighborhood around schools or other evacuation sites. Most states provide a mapping utility to locate sexual offenders. These maps often link to a database that provides name, address and photo of the convicted felon. It is important to identify these individuals and their proximity to the site. There are many documented cases of sexual predators using a crisis as an opportunity for sexual predation.

## ROUTE MAP CHECKLIST

These considerations should be included when mapping routes:

- Evacuation routes
- Incident Command Post locations
- Incoming district responder routes
- Incoming fire routes
- Incoming medical routes
- Outgoing medical routes
- Incoming parent routes
- Outgoing parent routes
- Staging area
- Landing zone
- Media staging
- Reunification signage locations
- Parent check-in location
- Possible road block sites
- Possible neighborhood evacuation perimeter
- Sexual offender locations
- Security perimeter
- Long perimeter

## NOTIFICATION PROCEDURES

In the event of a reunification, parent/guardian notification is a necessary first step. Many schools or districts have mass notification systems to bulk call and/or text information to the parent population. It is imperative that accurate, factual information be delivered, starting with the crucial First Message. While it may seem comforting to tell parents that everyone is okay, or to minimize the number of injuries, this First Message not only begins the recovery process, it may be evidentiary for purposes of liability. Rather than saying "All students are safe," it is probably more accurate to report that, "We are in the process of establishing the safety status of all students and staff."

With the number of cell phones available to ever younger student populations, parents will, in all likelihood, be the first to arrive at the impacted school. Prepare for the fact that this may occur prior to the transmission of any official notification by the school or the district.

Students will call or text their parents/guardians immediately during a crisis, despite school policy prohibiting mobile phone use. Additionally, some schools may not have accurate contact information for all parents. It may be possible during a crisis to leverage this to the school's advantage by writing out reunification information for the students to text to their parents/guardians.

Prepared notification language is vital. While anything written in advance may not exactly fit the circumstances of any given crisis, it may provide a valuable advantage in the initial phase of a crisis. These statements can be vetted with the district public information officer and legal counsel as part of the planning process. Other notifications should be considered. Contacting district legal counsel, as well as the district's insurance providers, should be part of the notification process.

## SPECIAL NEEDS CONSIDERATIONS

Schools are encouraging parents of students with special medication needs to consult their physicians about medication Go Kits. The medication Go Kit may include extra dosages that are not in the school medicine locker. If it's determined that the school does create a medication Go Kit, security and chain of custody should be part of the plan and procedure.

Other special needs considerations include mobility and care-taking. An evacuation and reunification can be especially disturbing and challenging for special needs students. The plan should consider staging special needs students apart from the general population to ensure adequate supervision and responsiveness.

## TIME OF DAY CONTINGENCIES

Time of day may impact how a reunification evolves. A crisis at the end of the day, when buses are already on site, may actually require a controlled release reunification. It is not beneficial to immediately release students who have witnessed a traumatic incident, even though the buses are there and it's the end of the school day. Mental health concerns might dictate a controlled release so that crisis counseling can be made available. This mandates a site plan that includes bus staging areas.

## PARENTS ARE CAPABLE

There may be circumstances where some of the early arrival parents can be given a task. This is situational, but consider that, when given a job, parents are now helping with the crisis. This has important psychological benefits in addition to distributing labor. "Can you help set up this table?" or "Could you help me by placing these signs along Elm street?" Both are necessary tasks, and can enlist the parent into being part of the solution.

## GO KITS FOR REUNIFICATION

Reunification Go Kits contain specialized items that are unique to the reunification process, such as caution tape, clip boards and pens, signage, and reunification cards). Consequently, these kits are different than school evacuation Go Kits. Since reunification is often managed by District personnel, reunification Go Kits aren't necessary at each school, rather the kits can stay with District response teams. Larger districts may have several kits, one at the district office and others in the trunks or backs of vehicles used by District responders. Smaller Districts may have only two kits. One at the District office, and one with the primary District responder. (Two is a suggested minimum: redundancy is important.) Inventories and locations should be audited once a quarter.

## THE REUNIFICATION OPERATION KIT

Available on the website are templates to create a Reunification Operation Kit.

## READY TO PRINT SIGNAGE

Available on the website are downloadable signs. These are sized at 24" x 32" comfortably fitting in most sandwich board curb sign frames.

# FAQs

## FREQUENTLY ASKED QUESTIONS

Since introducing the Standard Reunification Method in 2012, thousands of districts, departments and agencies have scrutinized, evaluated and ultimately implemented the program. During the process some questions seem to come up often.

## SERIOUSLY, WHAT DOES IT REALLY COST?

Since its introduction in 2009, public K12 schools, districts, departments and agencies were free to use The "I Love U Guys" Foundation programs at no cost.

In 2015, the Foundation expanded availability, and now offers the programs to any public or private organization at no charge. Simply download the materials and begin the process.

## DO WE NEED TO BUY TRAINING IN ORDER TO USE THE PROGRAMS?

No. We've attempted to put enough material online so that schools and law enforcement can successfully implement Foundation programs. We know of thousands of schools across the US and Canada that have implemented the programs using internal resources.

That said, part of our sustainability model relies not just on charitable giving, but in providing training for districts departments and agencies. If your organization is interested in Foundation training, please contact us for rates and terms.

## CAN I MODIFY MATERIALS?

Some details may need to be customized to your location. For instance, the classroom poster should be modified to include hazards and safety strategies that are specific to your location.

## ARE THE SOURCE MATERIALS AVAILABLE?

Yes. Some of the materials are available. Original, digital artwork can be provided to organizations that have signed a "Notice of Intent" or a "Memorandum of Understanding" with The "I Love U Guys" Foundation.

Please note: Currently, we are migrating from Pages on the Mac to QuarkXPress. (Adobe InDesign made our eyes bleed. Depending on the material original artwork is only provided in Mac OS X, Pages version 4.3 iWork '09.

## CAN YOU SEND ME MATERIALS IN MICROSOFT WORD?

Short answer, no. Retaining the graphic integrity of the materials proved beyond our capabilities using Microsoft Word.

## CAN I REALLY USE THE MATERIALS? WHAT ABOUT COPYRIGHTS AND TRADEMARKS?

Schools, districts, departments, agencies and organizations are free to use the materials under the "Terms of Use" outlined in this document.

## DO I NEED TO ASK PERMISSION TO USE THE MATERIALS?

No. You really don't need to ask permission. But, it would be fabulous if you let us know that you're using our programs.

## DO I HAVE TO SIGN AN MOU WITH THE FOUNDATION?

It is not necessary to sign an MOU with the Foundation. But, please consider it. The Foundation is committed to providing programs at no cost. Yet, program development, enhancement and support are cost centers for us. One way we fund those costs is through private grants and funding.

An MOU is a strong demonstration of program validity and assists us with these types of funding requests.

## DO I HAVE TO SEND A NOTICE OF INTENT?

In the absence of an MOU, a Notice of Intent provides similar value to us regarding demonstrations of program validity to potential funders.

## DO I HAVE TO NOTIFY YOU AT ALL THAT I AM USING THE SRM?

We often speak with school safety stakeholders that have implemented the SRP or SRM but hadn't quite mentioned it to us. Please, please, please let us know if your school, district, department or agency are using our programs.

It is our goal that the SRP and SRP become "Gold Standards." The more schools, districts, departments and agencies that we can show are using the program, the greater the chance for achieving our goal.

## CAN I PUT OUR LOGO ON YOUR MATERIALS?

Yes. But with some caveats. If you are a school, district, department or agency you may include your logo on posters and handouts. If you are a commercial enterprise, please contact us in advance with intended usage.

In some states we have co-branding agreements with "umbrella" organizations. In those states we ask that you also include the umbrella organizations branding.

Please see http://iloveuguys.org/cobranding for a list of current states and organizations.

## WE WOULD LIKE TO PUT THE MATERIALS ON OUR WEBSITE.

Communication with your community is important. While you are free to place any material on your website, it's preferable that you link to the materials from our website. The reason for this is to allow us to track material usage. We can then use these numbers when we seek funding.

But, don't let that be a show stopper. If your IT group prefers, just copy the materials to your site.

Made in the USA
Coppell, TX
08 June 2022

78575364R00031